THE WEST VIRGINIA

STATE OF WEST VIRGINIA.

JUNE 20 1863

MONTANI SEMPER LIBERI.

HAND BOOK

AND

IMMIGRANT'S GUIDE.

BY

J. H. DISS DEBAR,
Commissioner of Immigration for the State of West Virginia.

PARKERSBURG:
GIBBENS BROTHERS, JOB PRINTERS,
1870.

THE WEST VIRGINIA HAND-BOOK.

—AND—

IMMIGRANT'S GUIDE.

A SKETCH OF THE STATE OF WEST VIRGINIA.

Geographical Position, Historical Outline, State Constitution, Population, Surface and Soil, Agriculture, Stock-Farming, Woolgrowing, Fruit and Wine-growing, Timber, Coal, Iron, Petroleum, Salt and other Minerals, Manufacturing, Water Power, Internal Improvements, Education, Religious Worship, Lands and Farms, Titles and Prices, with a brief notice of each County, and an

OFFICIAL STATE DIRECTORY AND MAP.

BY

J. H. DISS DEBAR,
State Commissioner of Immigration.

Parkersburg:
GIBBENS BROS., JOB PRINTERS,
1870.

ERRATA.

—o—

Page 16 line 8 from below, for *Alleghany*, read Blue Ridge.
Page 33 line 14 from above, for *valley*, read Valley.
Page 100 line 16 from below, for *variety*, read Vineyard.
Page 128 line 15 from above, for 25, read 12.
Page 173 line 15 from above, for *valley*, read hill.
Page 178 line 20 from above, for 40, read 10.
Page 167, "Religious Worship", The figures given by the Census of 1860, indicate church accommodation, and not actual membership.

A few other Typographical errors and Omissions stand uncorrected.

PREFACE.

ON the 2d day of March 1864, the Legislature of West Virginia passed an Act "for the encouragement of immigration to this State," by virtue of which I received the appointment of Commissioner on the following day. Since then, in pursuance of said act, I have distributed in other States of the Union, and in Europe, upward of 18,000 pamphlets, hand-bills and advertisements, exhibiting the various resources of the State, and our inducements to immigration. One of the results of these publications, was an amount of inquiry from all those countries, which an unsalaried officer cannot be expected to answer satisfactorily by correspondence, and must be met with printed information more full than heretofore conveyed.

Though not claiming to be exhaustive upon a subject capable of filling volumes, this Manual possesses the merit of supplying, from a personal observation and professional experience of twenty-five years, that class of unvarnished facts and figures, which, in my official correspondence, forms the subject of the most general enquiry. It is hoped that its freedom from all romance and exaggeration may secure for it the attention and confidence of that class of honest and enterprising workers in both hemispheres, whom we are most anxious to welcome as permanent settlers to our infant State. J. H. D. D.

CONTENTS.

THE
GEOGRAPHICAL POSITION.

UNTIL the year 1863 the territory embraced within the present limits of West Virginia, and computed at about 26,000 square miles, was, with the exception of the six Potomac counties, known as the Western or Trans-Alleghany district of the State of Virginia. It is situated between North latitude 37, 30 and 40, 30, and West longitude 0.45 and 5.30 from Washington, and a legal description of its boundary would read about as follows:

Beginning near Harpers Ferry, at the point where the Blue Ridge is intersected by the Potomac river, thence, with said river and the North Branch thereof, to Fairfax's Stone, a corner of the State of Maryland, on the Backbone ridge of the Alleghany mountains, thence with a line of Maryland North to the Pennsylvania line, thence with this line West to the Southwest corner of Pennsylvania, thence with another line of that State North to Western bank of the Ohio river, thence with said bank and river to the mouth of Big Sandy river, a corner to the State of Kentucky, thence with said river to the mouth of Knox creek a corner of Virginia, Kentucky and West Virginia, thence with a line of and including the counties of McDowell and Mercer to the top of East river mountain, thence with said ridge and with Peters mountain to the Alleghany mountain, thence with the top of the same to the Haystack Knob, a corner of Virginia and West Virginia, thence with the Southern line of, and including, Pendleton county to the top of Great North or Shenandoah mountain, thence with the same and Branch mountain to a corner of Hardy and Rockingham counties, thence with lines of and including the counties of Hardy, Hampshire, Morgan, Berkeley and Jefferson to the beginning.

With the exception of the five counties last named, and the county of Pendleton, which are drained by the Potomac river and branches, the whole of West Virginia geographically belongs to the Great Mississippi Valley, all of her streams being more or less direct tributaries of the Ohio river which forms the western boundary of the State to an extent of 300 miles.

The name "*West* Virginia," though relatively proper, appears almost anomalous when the boundary above described is traced on a map of the United States, and the distances are measured to the great Eastern seaports and markets of the continent. This operation will show the distance from the East end of the State to be only 81 miles to Baltimore, 179 miles to Philadelphia, 286 to New York, and 540 to Boston; all these points being accessible by rail at an average rate of 25 miles per hour. From the White Sulphur Springs, in Greenbrier county, the Chesapeake & Ohio Railroad carries passengers to Norfolk, on the Atlantic, a distance of 330 miles in 16 hours, and when completed from the Springs westward, will accomplish the distance to Cincinnati in an equal space of time. From Parkersburg on the Ohio river, and western border of the State, Cincinnati is now reached by rail, 205 miles, in 9 hours, by river, 265 miles, in 20 hours. St. Louis by rail, 545 m., in 22 hours; Pittsburgh by rail, 260 m., in 11 hours, by river, 200 m., in 30 hours; New Orleans by river 6 days; Baltimore, the principal market of West Virginia, and nearest seaport by rail, 383 miles is reached in 16 hours. Washington, the capital of the United States, 405 miles, in 17 hours from the Western, and 5 hours from the Eastern end of the State.

Through the channel of the Ohio river, one of whose principal sources rises in the West Virginia mountains, the State is placed in direct communication with the markets of the far West and the Gulf of Mexico, and in fact with the trade of whole Mississippi Valley.

"The ploughs and automaton harvesters," says Mr. Dodge, "which will hereafter garner the wealth of western prairies may, be transported to all those plains in vessels fabricated by the labor of West Virginia from her own oak and iron, and the metal of those implements may be mined, the ore heated by adjacent strata of coal, the requisite flux obtained from the same hill, and all compacted into a perfect machine, with timber found growing on the surface, which has been manufactured by a perpetual water power that leaps the crags of the summit and falls gently into the vale below, meandering towards the Ohio river, quiet as the meditative ox that fattens on the sweetest of perennial herbage upon its banks."

Where in the wide world, lies so broad a network of water communication at the very foot of a State so full of the varied treasures of the forest and the mine. That such a country with an elevation above the malarias of the lowlands and never rising above the level of corn and sorghum production, within a few hours of the sea and its treasures and facilities for transit—a land peculiar for its green pastures flowing with milk, for its bright flowers laden with honey, and its river slopes that promise to run with wine—should lack inhabitants, or the hum of industry, or the show of wealth is an absurdity in the present and an impossibility in the future."

HISTORICAL AND POLITICAL OUTLINE.

To revert under this head to the early history of the Mother State beyond the causes which induced the separation, is not important for the purposes of this brief sketch.

The deep, fertile soil of Western Virginia had, long before the Revolution, attracted the attention of land speculators, and even George Washington, when engaged as a public surveyor west of the Alleghanies in 1750, could not refrain from entering and patenting on his own acconnt upwards of thirty-two thousand acres in the Ohio and Great Kanawha Valleys, which, though then in a state of unbroken wilderness, were valued in his will, in 1799, at $10 per acre.

No permanent settlement, however, appears to have been made in Western Virginia proper, until 1764, when John and Sam'l Pringle, deserters from Fort Pitt, located themselves at the mouth of Turkey Run, on the Buckhannon fork of the Valley river, in what is now the county of Upshur, and only a few miles above Phillippa, in Barbour county, which witnessed the first bloody engagement of the late rebellion. In 1768 these adventurous pioneers were followed by the Hackers, Sleeths the Hughe's of hunter's fame, and John Jackson and his sons, whose descendents have filled with distinction prominent positions at the bar and bench, in the army, and in the councils of the State and nation.

Among these pioneers and thousands of their immediate followers, few were actuated by higher motives than love of adventure, and the gratification of their immediate wants through the manly sports of the forest and mountain. Game and fish, and even wild fruit and honey were everywhere abundant, and the slovenly cultivation of a few half cleared acres in this genial climate, furnished in abundance the bread and other necessaries of the settler's frugal fare. Until the close of the last century, the new settlements being more or less exposed to the depredations of hostile Indians, the people felt little encouragement to increase or improve possessions held by so slender a tenure. While the constant struggle with adverse circumstances and the free intercourse with nature developed to an eminent degree the innate powers of mind and body, and the sturdy self-reliance proverbial in the American pioneer, this habit of living from hand to mouth, and the abnegation of all comforts not easily attainable, did perhaps as much as the institution of slavery, induce that lack of industrial enterprise and thrift which characterizes the "old stock" of West Virginians to the present day. In a community so sparsely scattered over a timbered wilderness, with few roads, and less schools and churches, the march of civilization was necessarily slow, in contrast with the Eastern section of the State, whose wealth, intelligence and consequent power, at an early day inclined to disregard the just claims of the humble

West, and fostered that inequality in taxation and in the distribution of internal improvements which led to political jealousy between the two sections, and other events aiding, to their final separation.

This solution of the difficulty was first timidly suggested more than thirty years ago, and probably involved then the Valley of Virginia, along with the Trans-Alleghany section, leaving the Blue Ridge as the boundary between the parts to be severed. But the pride and sensitiveness of the old Dominion on the subject of territorial integrity left no hope for the discontented spirits in the West, except in the bare possibilities of a distant future. It was reserved for a great national calamity to afford the long sought opportunity, which was improved in the nick of time, under the applause of the loyal nation, with a keener sense of expediency than of scrupulous constitutional proprieties.

On the 19th of April 1861, the ordinance was adopted by the Richmond Convention, declaring Virginia seceded from the Union. In this Assembly the western section of the old State was fully represented, but not unanimous in sentiment, a majority of her members voting against the ordinance. A thrill of unprecedented excitement shook the country from the Alleghanies to the Ohio river, when the western delegates returned home to denounce the insults and persecutions their fidelity to the Union had called upon their heads. A few days sufficed to fan the heartburnings of the past into a fierce revolutionary flame, and to arouse the proverbially equanimous people to prompt and energetic action.

The direction of this movement, so pregnant with momentous events, proceeded from the ancient town of Clarksburg, where nearly twelve hundred citizens assembled at the court-house upon a notice of forty-eight hours, on Monday April 22nd 1861, and the following preamble and resolutions were submitted by the leading spirit of the occasion, Hon. John S. Carlile, and adopted without one dissenting voice:

WHEREAS, the Convention now in session in this State, called by the Legislature, the members of which had been elected twenty months before said call, at a time when no such action as the assemblage of a Convention by legislative enactment was contemplated by the people, or expected by the members they elected in May, 1859, at which time no one anticipated the troubles recently brought upon our common country by the extraordinary action of the State authorities of South Carolina, Georgia, Alabama, Mississippi, Florida, Louisiana, and Texas, has, contrary to the expectation of a large majority of the people of this State, adopted an ordinance withdrawing Virginia from the Federal Union, and whereas, by the law calling said Convention, it is expressly declared that no such ordinance shall have force or effect, or be of binding obligation upon the people of this State, until the same shall be ratified by the voters at the polls; and, whereas, we have seen with regret that demonstrations of hostility unauthorized by law, and inconsistent with the duty of law-abiding citizens, still owing allegiance to the Federal Government, have been made by a portion of the people of this State against the said Government; and whereas, the Governor of this Commonwealth has, by proclamation, undertaken to decide for the people of Virginia, that which they had reserved to themselves, the right to decide by their votes at the polls, and has called upon the volunteer soldiery of this State to report to him and hold themselves in readiness to make war upon the Federal Government, which Government is Virginia's Government, and must in law and of right continue to to be, until the people of Virginia shall, by their votes, and through the ballot-box, that great conservator of a free people's liberties, decide otherwise: and, whereas, the peculiar situation of Northwestern Virginia, separated as it is, by natural barriers from the rest of the State, precludes all hope of timely succor in the hour of danger, from other portions of the State, and demands that we should look to and provide for our own safety in the fearful emergency in which we now find ourselves placed by the action of our State authorities, who have disregarded the great fundamental principle upon which our beautiful system of Government is based, to-wit: "That all Governmental power is derived from the consent of the governed;" and have, without consulting the people, placed this State in hostility to the Federal Government by seizing upon its ships and obstructing the channel at the mouth of Elizabeth river, by wresting from the Federal officers at Norfolk and Richmond the custom-houses, by tearing from the Nation's property the Nation's flag, and putting in its place a bunting, the emblem of rebellion, and by marching upon the National Armory at Harper's Ferry; thus inaugurating a war without consulting those in whose name they profess to act: and, whereas, the exposed condition of Northwestern Virginia requires that her people should be united in action, and harmonious in purpose—there being a perfect identity ef interests in times of war as well as in peace—therefore, be it

Resolved, That it be and is hereby recommended to the people in each and all of the counties composing Northwestern Virginia, to appoint delegates, not less than five in number, of their wisest, best, and discreetest men, to meet in Convention at Wheeling, on the 13th day of May next, to consult and determine upon such action as the people of Northwestern Virginia should take in the present fearful emergency.

Resolved, That Hon. John S. Carlile, W. P. Goff, Hon. Charles S. Lewis, John J. Davis, Thos. L. Moore, S. S. Flemming, Lot Bowen, Dr. Wm. Dunkin, Wm. E. Lyon, Felix Sturm, and James Lynch be and are hereby appointed delegates to represent this County in said Convention. JOHN HURSEY, President.

J. W. HARRIS, Secretary.

In response to this address delegates from twenty-five western counties met at Wheeling on the 13th of May, and passed resolutions denouncing the ordinance of secession as an act of treason, and providing for a Convention of all the counties of *Virginia* adhering to the National Government.

This Convention representing forty counties assembled at Wheeling on the 11th of June. Upon the principle that secession was void in law and the authority of the State resided in its loyal citizens, this body repudiated the acts of the Convention and authorities of Richmond, and proceeded to reorganize the lawful government of the State.

Though unequivocal in its professions of loyalty, this assembly contained but a small proportion of *original* freesoilers, abolitionists and New-State men. Yet even its moderate republicanism was in advance of the electoral majority of the counties wherein delegates had been appointed, with more or less irregularity. The vote cast was exceedingly small, at many precincts almost nominal. Twelve or more western counties were entirely unrepresented, and a number of members were admitted to seats in this and subsequent legislative bodies, upon no other credentials than their notoriety as *refugees*, homeless politicians, who were charitably permitted to mistake their personal wants for the popular will, and their private grudges for public interests.

To exalt and to glorify the "spontaneous outburst of West Virginia loyalty" through the press, on the stump and in the legislative halls, was then the *policy* of the hour. But eye witnesses cannot forget to what extent popular convictions vacillated in the breeze of current events, nor resist the presumption, that had the first half a dozen regiments that took possession of West Virginia soil worn the gray instead of the blue, the political status of this section of country might have been totally reversed.

The government elected by the people by authority of this Convention, with Hon. F. H. Pierpoint in the Executive chair, was bravely styled the "Reorganized Government of the State of Virginia," although its authority did not then extend over a single county East of the Alleghanies, and was warmly resisted in several counties of the West. This political arrangement, however, was necessary in order to comply with the provisions of the Federal Constitution requiring the consent of the Legislature of a State to the erection of a new State within its jurisdiction. During its first session the organized Legislature elected United States Senators, passed a law staying the collection of debts, and voted two hundred thousand dollars for the defence of the State and a like amount for civil purposes. It also issued a call for a New-State Constitutional Convention, which body was elected on the 24th of October, 1861, and inaugurated its labors at Wheeling on the 26th of November following.

At least one feature of the Constitution elaborated by this Convention failed to satisfy the friends of universal freedom. Human slavery remained unscathed, and not until after Congress had declined to recognize the new State upon those terms, the following compromise with expediency, known as the "Willey Amendment" was assented to by the people.

"The children of slaves born within the limits of this State after the fourth of July, eighteen hundred and sixty-three, shall be free; and all slaves within the said State who shall, at the time aforesaid, be under the age of ten years, shall be free when they arrive at the age of twenty-one years; and all slaves over ten and under twenty-one years shall be free when they arrive at the age of twenty-five years; and no slave shall be permitted to come into the State for permanent residence therein."

This lingering homage to a great national sin remained a part of the new State Constitution until the adoption of the 13th amendment to the Constitution of the United States, abolishing slavery throughout the land, and forever.

As a footprint of the march of ideas it may be noted here, that as late as the New State election in May, 1863, radical abolitionists were violently denounced and opposed, *within the republican ranks*, and generally defeated by men who, since then, fell into line with great exultation after the passage of the 13th Constitutional Amendmeut, and are now lustily cheering the fifteenth.

The consent of the Legislature of reorganized Virginia to the formation of the new State was given on 13th of May, 1862, and on the 31st of December following. President Lincoln approved the act of Congress admitting West Virginia into the Union to comprise the following forty-eight counties:

Hancock, Brooke, Ohio, Marshall, Wetzel, Marion, Monongalia, Preston, Taylor, Tyler, Pleasants, Ritchie, Doddridge, Harrison, Wood, Jackson, Wirt, Roane, Calhoun, Gilmer, Barbour, Tucker, Lewis, Braxton, Upshur, Randolph, Mason, Putnam, Kanawha, Clay, Nicholas, Cabell, Wayne, Boone, Logan, Wyoming, Mercer, McDowell, Webster, Pocahontas, Fayette, Raleigh, Greenbrier, Monroe, Pendleton, Hardy, Hampshire and Morgan.

The subsequent admission of the counties of Berkeley and Jefferson into the new State, though contested by the State of Virginia, will probably be finally confirmed by the Supreme Court of the United States. Since 1863 the following new counties were created by the acts of the Legislature:

Mineral out of Hampshire.

Grant out of Hardy.

Lincoln out of Boone and Cabell.

The new State Constitution, as amended, was adopted by the people on the 26th of March, 1863.

A general election for the new State government was held on the 28th of May and on the 20th of June, 1863, the State of West Virginia was solemnly inaugurated at Wheeling, by Hon. A. I. Boreman of Wood county, first Governor of the State, and the assembled Legislature. About the same time Gov. F. H. Pierpoint transferred the reorganized government of Virginia to Alexandria, Richmond being still at a rather inconvenient distance beyond the Federal lines.

EXTRACTS FROM THE CONSTITUTION OF WEST VIRGINIA.

Sec. 1. The State of West Virginia shall be and remain one of the United States of America. The Constitution of the United States, and the laws and treaties made in pursuance thereof shall be the supreme law of the land.

Sec. 2, Describes the boundaries of the State substantially as given page 1.

SEC. 3. Declares that the powers of government reside in all the citizens of the State, and can be rightfully exercised only in accordance with their will and appointment.

SEC. 6. Designates as citizens of West Virginia, the citizens of the United States residing in the State,

SEC. 7. Provides for equality of representation.

ARTICLE II—BILL OF RIGHTS.

I. The privilege of the writ of *habeas corpus* shall not be suspended except when in time of invasion, insurrection or other public danger, the public safety require it. No person shall be held to answer for treason, felony or other crime not cognizable by a justice, unless on presentment or indictment of a grand jury. No bill of attainder, *ex post facto* law, or law impairing the obligation of a contract, shall be passed.

No law abridging freedom of speech, or of the press shall be passed. Exceptions are made in case of obscene books, papers or pictures, and of libel and defamation of character. (Sec. 4.)

6. Private property shall not be taken for public use without just compensation. No person, in time of peace shall be deprived of life, liberty or property, without due process of law. The military shall be subordinate to the civil power.

7. In suits at common law, where the value in controversy exceeds twenty dollars, the right of trial by jury, if required by either party, shall be preserved. No fact tried by a jury shall be otherwise re-examined in any case than according to the rules of the common law.

9. No man shall be compelled to frequent or support any religious worship, place or ministry whatsoever; nor shall any man be enforced, restrained, molested or burthened in his body or goods, or otherwise suffer, on account of his religious opinions or belief; but all men shall be free to profess, and by argument to maintain, their opinions in matters of religion and the same shall in no wise affect, diminish or enlarge the civil capacities. And the Legislature shall not prescribe any re-

ligious test whatever; or confer any peculiar privileges or advantages on any sect or denomination; or pass any law requiring or authorizing any religious society, the people of any district within this State, to levy on themselves or others, any tax for the erection or or repair of any house for public worship, or for the support of any church or ministry; but it shall be left free to every person to select his religious instructor, and to make for his support such private contract as he shall please.

10. Treason against the State shall consist only in levying war against it, or in adhering to its enemies, giving them aid and comfort. No person shall be convicted of treason unless on the testimony of two witnesses to the same overt act, or on confession in open court. Treason shall be punished, according to the character of the acts committed, by the infliction of one or more of the penalties of death, imprisonment, fine, or confiscation of the real and personal property of the offender, as may be prescribed by law.

ARTICLE III—ELECTIONS AND OFFICERS.

White male citizens of the State alone entitled to vote. The fourth Thursday in Ootober is fixed for holding State and county elections, and the vote in the same to be by ballot, No person who is a minor, or of unsound mind, or a pauper, or under conviction of treason, felony or bribery in an election, or who has not been a resident of the State for one year, and of the county in which he offers to vote for thirty days next preceding the election, shall be permitted to vote while such disability continues.

11. Any citizen of this State, who shall, after the adoption of this Constitution, either in or out of the State, fight a duel with deadly weapons, or send or accept a challenge so to do; or who shall act as second, or knowingly assist in such duel, shall ever thereafter be incapable of holding any office of honor, trust or profit under this State.

12. The Legislature may provide for a registry of voters. They shall prescribe the manner of conducting

and making returns of elections, and of determining contested elections; and shall pass such laws as may be proper to prevent intimidation, disorder or violence at the polls, and corruption or fraud in voting.

ARTICLE IV.—LEGISLATURE.

1. The Legislative powers shall be vested in a Senate and House of Delegates.

3. The term of office of Senators shall be two years, and that of Delegates one year. The Senators first elected shall divide themselves into two classes, one Senator from every district being assigned to each class; and of these classes, the first, to be designated by lot in such manner as the Senate may determine, shall hold their offices for one year, and the second for two years; so that after the first election one-half of the Senators shall be elected annually.

4. For the election of Senators, the State shall be divided into nine Senatorial Districts; which number shall not be diminished, but may be increased as hereinafter provided.

6. Until the Senatorial Districts are altered by the Legislature, after the next census, they shall be composed as follows:

1st. Hancock, Brooke and Ohio.

2d. Marshall, Wetzel and Marion.

3d. Monongalia, Preston and Taylor.

4th. Pleasants, Tyler, Ritchie, Doddridge and Harrison.

5th. Wood, Jackson, Wirt, Roane, Calhoun and Gilmer.

6th. Barbour, Tucker, Lewis, Braxton, Upshur and Randolph.

7th. Mason, Putnam, Clay, Kanawha and Nicholas.

8th. Cabell, Wayne, Boone, Logan, Wyoming, Mercer and McDowell.

9th. Webster, Pocahontas, Fayette, Raleigh, Greenbrier and Monroe.

10th. Pendleton, Hardy, Hampshire and Morgan.

11th. Berkeley and Jefferson.

The apportionment of Delegates to the counties shall be as follows:

Barbour, Boone, Braxton, Brooke, Cabell, Doddridge, Fayette, Hancock, Jackson, Lewis, Logan, Hardy, Morgan, Mason, Mercer, Putnam, Ritchie, Roane, Tyler, Pendleton, Upshur, Wayne, Wetzel and Wirt, one delegate each.

To Harrison, Kanawha, Marion, Marshall, Hampshire, Monongalia, Preston, Jefferson and Berkeley, two delegates each.

To Ohio county, three delegates.

To Greenbrier and Monroe, together, three delegates.

To 1st Delegate District, Wood and Pleasants, together, two delegates.

2d. Calhoun and Gilmer, one delegate.

3d. Clay and Nicholas, one delegate.

4th. Webster and Pocahontas, one delegate.

5th. Tucker and Randolph, one delegate.

6th. Wyoming, Raleigh and McDowell, one delegate.

SEC. 11. Prescribes how often delegates are to be chosen from either county in the above six Districts, respective population being the basis of the scale of alternation.

20. The Legislature shall meet once in every year, and not oftener, unless convened by the Governor. The regular sessions shall begin on the third Tuesday in January, and Sec. 24. fixes the duration of the regular session at 45 days; not to be extended except with the concurrence of three-fourths of the members elected to each branch.

32. Fixes the compensation of Delegates and Senators, at $3 per diem. Presiding officers receive $2 per diem additional.

ARTICLE V—EXECUTIVE.

The chief executive power is vested in a Governor, elected by the voters of the State for the term of two years. Salary $2,000.

A Secretary of the State, Treasurer, Auditor and Atterney General are elected at the same time and for the same term as the Governor. Salary of Secretary, $1300;

Treasurer, $1400; Auditor, $1500. Salary of Attorney General as may be determined by law.

ARTICLE VI—JUDICIARY.

1. The Judiciary power of the State shall be vested in a Supreme Court of Appeals, and Circuit Courts, and such inferior tribunals as are herein authorized.

3. Divides the State into nine circuits. (By subsequent acts of the Legislature, under the Constitution, the number of circuits has been increased, as will be seen under the head of "Judicial Circuits" near the end of this volume.)

Judges are elected by the voters in their respective circuits, for the term of six years.

6. The circuit court shall have the supervision and control of all proceedings before Justices and other inferior tribunals, by *mandamus, prohibition or certiorari.* They shall, except in cases confided exclusively by this Constitution to some other tribunal, have original and general jurisdiction of all matters at law, where the amount in controversy, exclusive of interest, exceeds twenty dollars, and in all cases in equity, and of all crimes and misdemeanors. They shall have appellate jurisdiction in all cases civil and criminal, where an appeal, writ of error or supersedeas may be allowed to the judgment or proceedings of any inferior tribunal. They shall also have such other jurisdiction, whether supervisory, original, apellate or concurrent, as may be prescribed by law.

7. The Supreme Court of Appeals shall consist of three Judges, any two of whom shall be a quorum. They shall be elected by the voters of the State, and shall hold their offices for the term of twelve years; except that of those first elected, one, to be designated by lot in such a manner as they may determine, shall hold his office for four years; another, to be designated in like manner, for eight years; and the third for twelve years; so that one shall be elected every four years after the first election.

8. The Supreme Court of Appeals shall have original jurisdiction in cases of *habeas corpus*, *mandamus* and *prohibition*. It shall have appellate jurisdiction in civil cases where the matter in controversy, exclusive of costs, is of greater value or amount than two hundred dollars; in controversies concerning the titles or boundaries of land, the probate of wills, the appointment or qualification of a personal representative, guardian, committee, or curator, or concerning a mill, road, way, ferry, or landing, or the right of a corporation or county to levy tolls or taxes; and also in cases of *habeas corpus*, *mandamus* and *prohibition*, and cases involving freedom, or the constitutionality of a law. It shall have the appellate jurisdiction in criminal cases where there has been conviction for felony or misdemeanor in a circuit court, and such other appellate jurisdiction in both civil and criminal cases as may be prescribed by law.

ARTICLE VII—COUNTIES AND TOWNS.

Every county shall be divided into not less than three, nor more than ten townships, of not less than 400 hundred inhabitant each.

Townships elect annually, a Supervisor, Clerk, Surveyor of Roads, and every four years one or more Justices of the Peace, and every two years as many Constables as there are Justices in the township.

The Supervisors chosen in the townships of each county shall constitute the Board of Supervisors, and meet statedly at least four times a year. They shall elect one of their number President of the Board, and appoint a Clerk.

4. The Board of Supervisors of each County, a majority of whom shall be a quorum, shall, under such general regulations as may be prescribed by law, have the superintendence and administration of the internal affairs and fiscal concerns of their County, including the establishment and regulation of roads, public landings, ferries and mills; the granting of ordinary and other licenses; and the laying, collecting and disbursement of the county levies; but all writs of *ad quod damnum* shall issue from the Circuit Courts.

5. The voters of each county shall elect a Sheriff, Prosecuting Attorney, Surveyor of Lands, Recorder, one or more Assessors every two years. The Sheriff cannot be elected for two consecutive terms.

6. The Recorder, in addition to the duties incident to the recording of inventories, and other papers relating to estates, and of deeds and other writings, the registering of births, marriages and deaths, and the issuing of marriage licenses, shall have authority, under such regulations as may be prescribed by law, to receive proof of wills and admit them to probate, to appoint and qualify personal representatives, guardian, committees and curators, to administer oaths, take acknowledgements of deeds and other writings, and relinquishments of dower.

8. The civil jurisdiction of a Justice shall extend to actions of assumpsit, debt, detinue and trover, if the amount claimed, exclusive of interest, does not exceed one hundred dollars, when the defendant resides, or, being a non-resident of the State, is found, or has effects or estate within his township, or when the cause of action arose therein; but any other justice of the same county may issue a summons to the defendant to appear before the Justice of the proper township, which may be served by a constable of either township.

10. Either party to a civil suit brought before a Justice, where the value in controversy, or the damages claimed, exceeds twenty dollars; the defendant, in such cases of misdemeanor or breach of the peace as may be made by law cognizable by a single Justice, when the penalty is imprisonment or a fine exceeding five dollars, shall be entitled to a trial by six jurors, if demanded, under such regulations as may be prescribed by law.

11. In all cases an appeal shall lie, under such regulation as may be prescribed by law, from the judgment or proceedings of a Justice or Recorder, to the Circuit Court of the county, excepting judgment of Justices in assumpsit, debt, detinue and trover, and for fines, where the amount does not exceed ten dollars exclusive of interest and costs, and where the case does not involve

the freedom of a person, the validity of a law, or the right of a corporation or county to levy tolls or taxes.

ARTICLE VII—TAXATION AND FINANCE.

1. Taxation shall be equal and uniform throughout the State, and all property, both real and personal, shall be taxed in proportion to its value, to be ascertained as directed by law. No one species of property from which a tax may be collected, shall be taxed higher than any other species of property of equal value; but property used for educational, literary, scientific, religious or charitable purposes, and public property, may, by law, be exempted from taxation.

5. A capitation tax of one dollar shall be levied upon each white male inhabitant who has attained the age of twenty-one years.

8. The Legislature shall provide for an annual tax sufficient to defray the expenses of the State for one year; and for any deficiency that may have occurred during the preceding year.

5. No debt shall be contracted by this State except to meet casual deficits in the revenue, to redeem a previous liability of the State, to suppress insurrection, repel invasion or defend the State in time of war.

8. An equitable proportion of the public debt of Virginia, prior to 1861, to be ascertained by the Legislature, shall be assumed by this State, and to be redeemed within thirty-four years.

ARTICLE IX—FORFEITED AND UNAPPROPRIATED LANDS.

1. All private rights and interests in lands in this State, derived from, or under the laws of the State of Virginia prior to the time this Constitution goes into operation, shall remain valid and secure, and shall be determined by the laws heretofore in force in the State of Virginia.

2. No entry by warrant on land shall be hereafter made, and in all cases where an entry has been heretofore made and has been or shall be so perfected as to entitle the locator to a grant, the Legislature shall make provision by law for issuing the same.

ARTICLE X—EDUCATION.

1. All money accruing to this State, being the proceeds of forteited, delinquent, waste and unappropriated lands; and of lands heretofore sold for taxes and purchased by the State of Virginia, if hereafter redeemed, or sold to others than this State; all grants, devises or bequests that may be made to this State for the purposes of education or where the purposes of such grants, devises or bequests are not specified; this State's just share of the Literary Fund of Virginia, whether paid over or otherwise liquidated, and any sums of money, stocks and property which this State shall have the right to claim from Virginia for educational purposes; the proceeds of the estates of all persons who may die without leaving a will or heir, and of all escheated lands; the proceeds of any taxes that may be levied on the revenues of any corporation hereafter created; all monies that my be paid in as an equivalent for exemption from military duty; and such sums as may be apportioned by the Legislature for the purpose, shall be set apart as a separate fund, to be called the School Fund, and invested under such regulations as may be prescribed by law, in the interest bearing securities of the United States, or of this State; and the interest thereof shall be annually applied to the support of free schools throughout the State, and to no other purpose whatever. But any portion of said interest remaining unexpended at the close of a fiscal year, shall be added to, and remain a part of, the capital of the School Fund.

2. The Legislature shall provide, as soon as practicable, for the establishment of a thorough and efficient system of free schools. They shall provide for the support of such schools by appropriating thereto the interest of the invested school fund; the net proceeds of all forfeitures, confiscations and fines accruing to this State under the laws thereof; and by general taxation on persons and property, or otherwise. They shall also provide for raising, in each township, by the authority of the people thereof, such a proportion of

the amount required for the support of free schools therein as shall be prescribed by general laws.

3. Provisions may be made by law for the election and prescribing powers, duties, and compensation of a General Superintendent of free schools for the State, whose term of office shall be the same as that of the Governor; and for the election, in the several townships, by the voters thereof, of such officers, not specified by this Constitution, as may be necessary to carry out the objects of this article; and for the organization, whenever it may be deemed expedient, of a State Board of Instruction.

4. The Legislature shall foster and encourage moral, intellectual, scientific and agricultural improvement; they shall, whenever it may be practicable, make suitable provision for the blind, mute and insane, and for the organization of such institutions of learning as the best interests of general education in the State may demand.

ARTICLE XI—MISCELLANEOUS.

1. No lottery shall be authorized by law; and the buying, selling or transferring tickets or chances in any lottery shall be prohibited.

2. No charter of incorporation shall be granted to any church or religious denomination. Provisions may be made by general laws securing the title to church property, so that it shall be held and used for the purposes intended.

5. The Legislature shall pass general laws whereby any number of persons associated for mining, manufacturing, insuring or other purpose useful to the public, excepting banks of circulation and the construction of works of internal improvement, may become a corporation, on complying with the terms and conditions thereby prescribed; and no special act incorporating, or granting peculiar privileges to any joint stock company or

association, not having in view the issuing of bills to circulate as money or the construction of some work of internal improvement, shall be passed. No company or association, authorized by this section, shall issue bills to circulate as money. No charter of incorporation shall be granted under such general laws, unless the right be reserved to alter and amend such charter at the pleasure of the Legislature, to be declared by general laws. No act to incorporate any bank of circulation or internal improvement company, or to confer additional privileges on the same, shall be passed, unless public notice of the intended application for such act be given under such regulations as shall be prescribed by law.

ARTICLE XII—AMENDMENTS.

When any amendments to the Constitution are proposed the Legislature shall first submit to the people the question of calling a Convention. A majority of the votes of the State is required to authorize a Convention. And no acts of such Convention are valid until again ratified by the vote of the people.

Or when a proposed amendment be adopted by two successive legislatures after due publication in the newspapers in the State, it may be submitted to the vote of the people and shall be in force as soon as ratified by a majority of such vote.

POPULATION.

The last census previous to the division of the State of Virginia was taken in 1860, one year before the East and West virtually severed their political connection. As the paths of the two sections in the field of material progress may diverge more or less in the future, it will be of interest to note the condition of each at and before the time of separation.

Virginia, up to the formation of the new State, contained an area of 61,352 square miles or 40,000,000 acres, the following table exhibits the number of her whole population, white, free colored, and slave at every census, the total increase of each decade, per cent. and the number of souls per square mile.

Year	White Inhabitants	Free Colored.	Slaves	Aggregate	Total incr'se Per Cent.	Inhabitants per square m.
1790	442,113	12,766	293,427	748,303		11.66
1800	514,280	20,124	345,796	880,200	17.62	13.75
1810	551,534	30,570	392,518	974,622	10.72	15.22
1820	603,087	36,689	425,153	1,065,379	9.31	16.64
1830	694,300	47,348	469,757	1,211,405	13.70	18.94
1840	740,858	49,852	449,087	1,239,797	2.34	19.37
1850	894,800	54,333	472,528	1,421,661	14.66	20.65
1860	1,047,299	58,164	490,865	1,596,318	12.28	24.40

In 1860 the population of the counties now remaining in the mother State, over a surface of 35,000 square miles was

White.	Free Colored.	Slave.	Total Population.
691,773	55,373	472,494	1,219,640

and the population of the counties now embraced in West Virginia over a surface of 26,000 square miles, is given in the following table, exhibiting also the rate of white increase in each county from 1850 to 1860.

NOTE.—The eight counties designated as new in the following table having all been created since the Census of 1850, their population, in computing the rate of increase, should be credited to the old counties from which they were respectively taken. Though there are no data showing the exact proportion of population furnished by each of the old counties, it may answer a partial purpose to state, that Calhoun was principally taken from Gilmer, Clay from Nicholas and Braxton, Pleasants from Wood and Tyler, Roane from Jackson and Kanawha, McDowell from Logan, while Lewis furnished the greater part of the populous county of Upshur, and Randolph a portion of Upshur and the entire counties of Tucker and Webster. Jefferson is the only county showing a decrease not resulting from subdivision. This county, situated at the extreme eastern end of the State, contained nearly one-fifth of the whole slave population of West Virginia.

Rank in scale of white increase.	COUNTIES.	White.	Free Colored	Slave...........	Total...........	White incr'se per centum, since 1850.....
39	Barbour	8,728	135	95	8,958	2.23
27	Berkeley	10,589	286	1650	12,525	14.40
7	Boone	4,681	1	158	4,840	53.30
22	Braxton	4,885	3	104	4,992	18.42
29	Brooke	5,425	51	18	5,494	12 28
12	Cabell	7,691	24	305	8,020	30.40
	Calhoun (new)	2.492	1	9	2.502	
	Clay (new)	1,761	5	21	1,787	
2	Doddridge	5,168	1	34	5.203	90.10
8	Fayette	5,716	10	271	5,997	51.20
32	Gilmer	3.685	22	52	3,759	8.30
17	Greenbrier	10,500	186	1525	12,211	22.81
20	Hampshire	12,478	222	1213	13,913	00.80
31	Hancock	4,442	1	2	4,445	10.00
34	Hardy	8,521	270	1073	9.864	7.50
23	Harrison	13,176	32	582	13,790	17.50
15	Jackson	8,240	11	55	8,306	27.10
4 p. c't. dec'r.	Jefferson	10,064	511	3960	14,535	
26	Kanawha	13,785	181	2184	16,150	14.86
20 p. c't. d'c'r.	Lewis	7,736	33	230	7,999	
11	Logan	4,789	1	148	4,938	35.55
19	Marion	12,656	3	63	12,722	21.22
13	Marshall	12,911	57	29	12,997	28.44
14	Mason	8,750	47	376	9,173	27.70
5	Mercer	6,428	29	362	6,819	60.00
35	Monongalia	12,901	46	101	13,048	7.40
37	Monroe	9,536	107	1114	10,757	5.23
36	Morgan	3,614	24	94	3.732	5.64
	McDowell (new)	1,535			1,535	
24	Nicholas	4,471	2	154	4,627	15.22
16	Ohio	22,196	126	100	22,422	26.05
33	Pendleton	5,870	50	244	6,164	7.84
30	Pocahontas	3,686	20	252	3,958	11.59
25	Preston	13.182	63	67	13,312	14.88
18	Putnam	5,708	13	580	6,301	21.62
	Pleasants (new)	2,925	5	15	2,945	
1	Raleigh	3,291	19	57	3,367	90.34
38	Randolph	4,793	14	183	4,990	4.38
4	Ritchie	6,809		38	6,847	75.33
	Roane (new)	5,307	2	72	5,381	
10	Taylor	7,300	51	112	7,463	42.30
	Tucker (new)	1,392	16	20	1,428	
21	Tyler	6,488	11	18	6,517	18.97
	Upshur (new)	7,064	16	212	7,292	
9	Wayne	6,604		143	6,747	44.73
	Webster (new)	1,552		3	1,555	
6	Wetzel	6,691	2	10	6,703	54.64
28	Wirt	3,728		23	3,751	12.52
20	Wood	10,791	79	176	11,046	19.79
3	Wyoming	2,795	2	64	28,61	76.68
		355,526	2,791	18,371	376,688	
	Census of 1850.	278,641	2,082	20,500	301,223	
		76,885	709	2129	75,465	

White increase 27.23, free col'd 34, slave decr. 10.38, total incr. 25.50 per cent.

The foregoing table, carefully compiled from the United States Census shows the white increase of what is now the State of West Virginia for the decade ending in 1860 to have been 78,885 white, or 27.23 per cent. while that of the whole State of Virginia during the same period was only 152,499 souls or 17.40 per cent., leaving in favor of the West, an excess of nearly 10 per cent. over the average increase of both sections.

But the difference of progression becomes still more apparent by comparison between the increases of each separate section. Thus the white population of Eastern Virginia numbered in 1860 691,773

In 1850 616,159

Showing an increase of 75,614

or 12,27 per cent., which is less than half the ratio of increase of the Western section.

This fact taken in connection with the inferior improvement of the West, and the formerly litigious condition of the land titles, furnishes the measure of her superior natural advantages, and of what she may accomplish as a sovereign State under a wise and liberal administration.

Other facts may be learned, and inferences drawn from this table. Excepting Mercer, the ten counties first in rank in the scale of increase being of comparatively recent creation, it is evident that the erection of county towns, the improvement of roads and other conveniences contingent upon such subdivision, induce population to sections, which, as remote portions of large counties, possess little or no attraction. It follows that the objection to the formation of new counties, upon the sole ground of increased taxation for public improvements, is not well founded, since the burden is invariably shared by an immediate increase of new settlers.

Allowing 26,000 square miles to be the exact area of West Virginia, her population in 1860 was 14.48 inhabitants per square mile.

The last message of Governor Boreman alludes to an accession of 50,000 inhabitants since the inauguration of the new State, or an average increase of 1000 per county. If these figures refer to immigration alone, they are undoubtedly too large, but if including natural increase also, they will fall somewhat below the facts. In a healthy country like West Virginia, the natural increase, after deducting natural mortality, may be assumed at 2.50 per cent. per annum, which for the decade ending in 1870, would give 94,170 and swell the total population of the State to about 470,000. To this must be added the gains by immigration, after deducting the extraordinary mortality of the late war, and the losses by emigration lately increased by political causes.

The original settlers of Western Virginia emigrated principally from the eastern and valley sections of the State, and from Maryland and New Jersey. Their ancestry was generally traced to Great Britain and Northern Ireland, and though in several of the mountain counties a strong admixture of Pennsylvania German blood is still perceptible, yet the blending of races through several generations has resulted in a well defined anglo-saxon type, slightly modified by that Celtic ease of manner peculiar to the dwellers of a mild and fruitful climate. The genuine rural West Virginian is not much addicted to precipitous motion, rarely loses his temper or self-possession, and beyond the acquisition of the necessaries of life, limited by almost Spartan frugality, is disposed to leave the improvement of things around him to time and chance. This unprogressive disposition is the more striking, as his native intellect and sagacity are extraordinary and susceptible of high development under proper direction or the stimulus of personal ambition. Perhaps nowhere on the continent are there such treasures of natural power buried under the rust of indolence and prejudice, and at the same time such a display of urbanity and hospitality prompted by native tact and geniality. The political differences, private feuds and various changes consequent upon the late civil strife, may have left their mark upon the traditional virtues of West Virginians, yet enough survives of these to suggest a favorable contrast with popular manners in States North and West of us. Very unlike the proverbial Jonathan, the West Virginian seldom inquires into his neighbors business with indelcate curiosity, and no matter how strong or antagonistic his convictions, never intrudes them upon strangers in aggressive or controversial discourse.

Yet, to presume from these amiable traits upon an unlimited dose of meekness in the West Virginia mountaineer would be a serious mistake. His self-esteem is not by far the least prominent of his characteristics, and insults, even more than injuries, are quickly resented. The history of the late war teems with feats of West Virginia valor; both armies counted her sons by thousands, and among them not a few distinguished leaders, and heroes of the rank and file. On many a memorable field, schoolmates, friends, relatives, nay, brothers, met face to face under the deadly fire, always true to their cause and worthy of each others steel.

Nor is the geniality of the West Virginian permitted to temper his acuteness in matters of business, when business there is. While he seldom steps out of a leisurely walk in the pursuit of worldly lucre, he watches his personal interests with an eye that kindles up never more brightly behind its drowsy lashes, than when a chance for a *trade* or a speculation comes within reach. Then quickly his dormant faculties are aroused and concentrated upon the point—vital to his fame no less than to his purse—how to get the best of the bargain; and whether the object of barter be a horse or a saddle, an ox or a gun, a house or a farm, the principle "your eyes *is* your market" is strictly kept in view and a bargain once struck is seldom rued, except for a consideration. Many a cunning speculator whose laurels were conquered in Wall Street or in more northern latitudes, after plying his arts among our homespun population, recrossed the Alleghanies a wiser and a *lighter* man.

The foreign element of recent immigration is already quite numerously represented in different sections of the State. The total number of persons born in foreign countries is given in the Census of 1860 at 15,960, and by counties as follows:

Barbour	101	Jefferson	361	Putnam	70
Berkeley	630	Kanawha	372	Pleasants	55
Boone	143	Lewis	549	Raleigh	10
Braxton	67	Logan	13	Randolph	100
Brooke	450	Marion	308	Ritchie	258
Cabell	157	Marshall	357	Roane	26
Calhoun	16	Mason	1194	Taylor	391
Clay	—	Monroe	87	Tucker	34
Doddridge,	273	Mercer	52	Tyler	108
Fayette	29	Monongalia	160	Upshur	110
Gilmer	45	Morgan	85	Wayne	27
Greenbrier	491	McDowell	4	Webster	1
Hampshire	451	Nicholas	76	Wetzel	254
Hancock	336	Ohio	5511	Wood	708
Hardy	136	Pendleton	5	Wyoming	1
Harrison	301	Pocahontas	69	Wirt	21
Jackson	187	Preston	770		

In the absence of official data for the increase since 1860, no accurate estimate can be formed, though from such information as is accessible, it is supposed to exceed 4000, thus swelling the aggregate foreign born population of West Virginia to about 20,000 souls.

Of this number six-tenths are probably natives of the German States and Switzerland, three-tenths of Ireland, and the remainder of England, Scotland, Belgium, France, Denmark and Sweden.

CLIMATE.

Alike free from extremes of cold and heat, of rain and drought, and at an elevation inaccessible to malaria, West Virginia enjoys a climate unsurpassed, if equaled, by that of any other State. Indeed, not another area of 26,000 miles exists in the Mississippi Valley, so free from disease of any kind, and requiring so little from man or beast for the protection of health. Gastric and pulmonary patients from other States annually resort to our highland air and mineral springs in large numbers, to renovate the juices of life, and nurse their returning strength in the sports of our streams and forests. Permanent settlers, who came here with constitutions seriously impaired, have, after a few years, entirely recovered original vigor, and would not again exchange climate for any consideration.

From all that has been written and published about West Virginia, the above facts should be sufficiently notorious to dispense with sanitary statistics; yet, judging from official correspondence, localities are by no means rare where not only the social and political, but also the physicial circumstances of West Virginia are confounded with those of the mother State, Virginia. Distant inquirers who heard of the chills and fever of the lowlands of the East, are slow to realize that ague is a physical impossibility in our well drained valleys, sloping uninterruptedly from the lap of the Alleghany mountains towards the Potomac and Ohio rivers.

Although embracing in its longest diameter over three degrees of latitude, the difference in the vegetation is scarcely noticed. The same timber and crops found in the valleys of Preston, flourish on the hilltops of Wyoming and McDowell, while, excepting an imperfect specimen of cotton, nothing is produced in the latter counties, that does not thrive nearly as well at the other end of the State. But the great difference of altitude in an Eastern and Western direction, renders it necessary to consider the climate under three separate division, as follows:

1st. The mountain counties.

2d. The Ohio Valley section.

3d. The Lower Potomac counties.

Let the reader turn to the map and follow, the backbone of the Alleghanies northward, from the southern line of the State, in the county of Monroe. At the point where the East river mountains or Peters mountains connect with the backbone, the elevation of the latter is 2,650 feet. Opposite the White Sulphur Springs at the crossing of the Covington road 2000 feet. Source of Cheat and Greenbrier rivers, in Randolph county

2400 feet. Fairfax stone, corner of Maryland and West Virginia 2300, and at the crossing of the Baltimore & Ohio railroad 2620 feet. The main Alleghany ridge therefore presents the highest levels in the State. Almost parallel to it, and distant from 20 to 40 miles to the West, runs what is properly a continuation of the Cumberland mountains, but known at different points as Tug ridge, Flat top, Cotton hill, Gauley mountain, Rich mountain and Laurel hill, embracing the counties of Mercer, Monroe, Greenbrier, Pocahontas, Randolph, Tucker and Preston, and portions of Raleigh. Fayette and Nicholas. The seven counties first named, together with Pendleton, Hardy and Hampshire are generally designated as the *mountain group*, whose climate and temperature, as differing from the sections immediately East and West of it, are materially determined by superior altitude.

This group embraces the summit, plateaux, or table lands of West Virginia, its lowest valleys—the Potomac East and Tygart's river West of the Alleghanies—being not less than 1000 feet above tide water. The altitude of Cheat river valleys is given at 1375 feet, mouth of Greenbrier river 1333 feet, head of Elk and Buckhannon rivers 950 feet. The relative elevation of this section becomes apparent when it is stated that the level of the Ohio river above tide water is

At the Pennsylvania line	675 feet.
At Parkersburg	625 "
At the mouth of Great Kanawha	560 "

Average difference between the Ohio bottom and the lowest mountain valleys 400 feet.
The highest table lands 1800 "

The greatest difference between the arable levels *within* the mountain group is 1400 feet, which admits of considerable variation of climate and production.

Upon ascending into this upland region, the traveler, not entirely absorbed by the novelty and grandeur of its almost primeval scenery,, is immediately impressed with the singular dryness and purity of the atmosphere, the chrystalline limpidity of the springs and streams, and the tonic, bracing effect of the mountain air at all seasons of the year. The sensation first experienced here by the lowland dweller has been described as one of singular buoyancy of spirit, of sudden relief from the cares of health and the fears of premature death, and in truth, the most remarkable instances of human contentment and longevity in the State, are found in the settlements of this mountain range.

Inquiries in regard to the vegetation peculiar to this section, are generally answered from local sources so as to leave the impression, that its agricultural productions are identical with those or the remainder of the State, a statement which should be taken with some allowance. In regard to the counties of Greenbrier, Raleigh and parts of Nicholas and Pocahontas it is measurably true. Corn, sorghum and fruit, especially the grape—all of which crops are fair criterions of temperature, other things being equal—ripen sufficiently early to escape the first fall frosts. Not so, however, in the other sections of the mountain group, especially those lying more than 1200 feet above tide water. On the table lands of Nicholas, Webster, Tucker, Randolph and the Preston Glades, corn is an *uncertain* crop, and only the smaller or flint varieties, maturing within 100 days of planting time, may be relied upon. Fruit, such as apples and peaches, especially northern varieties, adapts itself promptly to the climate; and though the bloom may be retarded somewhat in the spring, the summer season is amply sufficient to perfect maturity. The Fox grape, and one or two inferior varieties are found growing wild and even luxuriantly on different levels of this section, but until more thorough experiments are made with improved varieties, it is likely that only the Concord, Hartford Prolific, Norton's Virginia Seedling, and others of equal hardiness, would thrive here with average success.

On the other hand the field and garden vegetables belonging to this latitude attain perfection without much regard to elevation, while to small grain and grass the climate is even more propitious than in the lower sections of the State. Snow falls here, generally as early as November, of sufficient depth to protect grass and small grain against hard frost throughout the season; and when, with the final thaw in March, fields and meadows emerge from their winter shroud, the luxuriant growth and dazzling verdure are surprising to behold.

Where pasture has been economized in the fall, cattle are generally turned upon grass toward the end of March, and remain out until November; yet the average period of winter feeding in this region should not be reckoned at less than six months, while the new settler not yet provided with pasture, and dependent solely upon summering in the woods, should store up forage for seven months at least.

The following table shows the mean temperature for each month of 1857, of Greenbrier county in the mountain group, with records of two other points in the State, and of Philadelphia and Cincinnati for comparison. Of the summit lands farther North no records of temperature could be procured.

MONTH.	W. Virginia Doddridge County.	W. Virginia, Kanawha County.	W. Virginia Greenbrier County.	Pennsylvania Philadelphia.	Ohio. Cincinnati.
January	29.40	35.14	32.55	30.79	36.11
February	36.20	41.69	38.40	36.44	40.32
March	46.30	51.58	47.68	48.12	50.19
April	51.20	53.98	51.96	50.28	52.37
May	68.15	65.62	68.03	64.65	70.03
June	70 85	68.51	69.93	70.65	72.87
July	75.42	74.67	75.93	76·00	79.52
August	76.28	73.38	74.33	74.53	75.64
September	63.50	65.93	61.29	66.18	68.36
October	49.35	50.99	48.35	52.32	54.37
November	43.24	46.91	44.23	47.49	49.30
December	33.85	34.97	33.33	33.00	30.18

THE OHIO VALLEY SECTION

comprises all that portion of the State lying between the mountain group and the Ohio river, to which all its numerous streams are more or less direct tributaries.

The level of this section, representing the mean elevation of the State, is said to vary from 600 to 1300 feet above tide water. Descending from the table lands westward, the country rapidly loses the character of mountain land. For a short distance the crystal brooks, still leaping from bench to bench, hasten merrily along. But so soon as the general level of the valleys is attained, the stream becomes slightly tinged with the hues of its rich alluvial banks, the current flows more gently, and the Ohio river finally reached with only an occasional ripple to mark the gradual decline. Thus the Little Kanawha meanders across the whole of this sloping region with an average fall of less than six feet per mile, while the descent of the Great Kanawha from Charleston to its mouth does not amount to one foot per mile.

The difference in the seasons between the extreme levels, amounts to about two weeks in point of time, and is most easily noticed in its gradual stages by the traveler crossing the State in an eastern or western direction, when the forest and meadow resume the garb of returning spring or fall.

"The mean temperature of West Virginia for the year," says Mr. Dodge, "as may be seen by examination of the isothermal lines, is lower than in any other locality in the same latitude East of the Missouri river. It lies between the lines of fifty degrees and fifty-four degrees, which embrace the Southern and central portions of Ohio, Indiana and Illinois, with contiguous portions of Missouri and Iowa; on the Atlantic deflecting northward to include the coast line between New York and Baltimore. The isothermal indicating a mean temperature of fifty-five degrees, passes through Baltimore and Washington, circles round the southern boundary of West Virginia, intersects the northern border of Kentucky and strikes St. Louis, leaving Philadelphia a very little north of the line. The line of fifty-two degrees would come very near the center of West Virginia. This would make the average temperature slightly lower than that of these two cities," and, it might be added dispel, another prejudice attributing to West Virginia a southern climate uncongenial to northern industry."

For the benefit of a numerous class of practical inquirers contemplating emigration, the following table was prepared from a diary kept during sixteen years in the county of Doddridge, very near the geographical center of the State. The year 1853 was selected as presenting the fullest record, and being a fair average year, so far as crops are concerned, the winter being perhaps of more than average severity :

METEOROLOGICAL TABLE.

	JANUARY.		FEBRUARY.		MARCH.		APRIL.	
1	Fair	22	Fair	25.44	Fair	38	Fair	74
2	Cloudy	32	Cloudy	29.52	"	40	Cloudy	58
3	"	30	Rain	42	"	38	Rain	56
4	Snow	31	"	56	Snow	36	"	42
5	Fair	28	"	58	Cloudy	44	Fair	52
6	"	26	"	38	Fair	32	Rain	50
7	"	30	Snow	36	"	30	Fair	52
8	"	28	Fair	26.36	Rainy	44	"	62
9	Cloudy	34	"	22	Snow	36	"	62
10	Windy	29	"	18	Cloudy	42	"	54
11	Snow	28	Snow	26	Rain	48	"	62
12	Clear	24	Fair	36	Cloudy	46	"	63
13	"	30	Cloudy	38	Fair	39	Cloudy	64
14	"	36	Fair	22.32	"	34.40	Rain	56
15	R'n & S'w	38	"	20	"	23,34	Fair	56
16	Fair	28	Rainy	21	"	23.40	Rain	58
17	"	29	Fair	28	Cloudy	42	"	56
18	Snow	24	Cloudy	34	Rain	44	Fair	56
19	Fair	20	"	34	Fair	40.59	Rain	54
20	"	20	Fair	18.36	"	28,56	Fair	57
21	"	20	Cloudy	20	Rain	48.60	"	72
22	Cloudy	28	Rainy	38.50	Fair	46.59	"	74
23	"	30	Snow	38	Cloudy	40	Rain	74
24	Snow	33	"	30	Fair	40.51	Cloudy	70
25	"	34	Fair	18	Cloudy	30.58	Rain	58
26	"	16	Snow	36	Rain	46	Fair	58
27	Fair	°.14	Rainy	45	Cloudy	48.40	"	70
28	"	10.34	Fair	54.64	C'd & F'r	30	"	60.75
29	"	10			"	42	Rain	78
30	"	20			"	60	Fair	70
31	"	25.44			"	54.66		

METEOROLOGICAL TABLE.—Continued.

	May.		June.		July.		August.	
1	Fair	70	Fair	70	Fair	92	Fair	80
2	Rain	71	"	76	"	92	Rain	78
3	Fair	72	"	82	Rain	88	"	78
4	Rain	78	"	82	"	86	"	76
5	"	70	Sultry	85	Cloudy	84	Cloudy	78
6	Fair	72	Showery	83	Fair	86	Fair	78
7	"	70	Fair	86	"	84	Rain	80
8	Rain	70	"	82	"	86	"	82
9	Fair	78	"	78	"	84	Fair	86
10	"	56	"	82	Showery.	86	"	88
11	"	63	"	84	Cloudy	84	"	87
12	Rain	62	"	85	Fair	86	"	90
13	"	61	"	86	"	78	"	92
14	Fair	66	"	86	"	80	"	92
15	"	80	"	88	Cloudy	74	"	92
16	"	80	"	87	Fair	71	"	86
17	Rain	83	"	85	"	78	"	80
18	"	82	"	89	"	78	"	82
19	Cloudy	58	"	89	Rain	80	"	72
20	Fair	60	Cloudy	88	"	72	"	76
21	"	70	Rain	86	"	68	"	79
22	"	78	Fair	52	Fair	75	"	80
23	Rain	54	"	52	"	74	"	78
24	Fair	54	"	74	"	76	Rain	80
25	Rain	60	"	72	Rain	78	Fair	79
26	Fair	64	"	80	"	72	"	75
27	Rain	69	Cloudy	84	Cloudy	73	Showery	74
28	Fair	72	"	87	"	72	Fair	75
29	"	74	"	89	"	72	"	72
30	"	71	Fair	90	"	78	"	80
31	"	75			"	76	"	84

NOTE.—The changes from rain to snow or hard frost, during the winter months, are often preceded by more or less wind, lasting from six to twenty-four hours. The most presistent winds prevail in March, and both equinoxes are generally heralded by storms. March 1853 counted eleven, and September seven windy days. West, northwest and southwest predominant. East and southeast winds occur more seldom and always bring foul weather. Summer showers and thunder storms generally come from the southwest.

The temperature of summer nights averages 20—30° below noon heat. Uncomfortably warm nights are rare, even in the Ohio and Kanawha Valleys, and almost totally unknown east of a line fifty miles east of, and parallel with the Ohio river.

METEOROLOGICAL TABLE,—Continued.

	SEPTEMBER.		OCTOBER.		NOVEMBER.		DECEMBER.	
1	Rain	78	Rain	66	Fair	36.48	Cloudy	44
2	"	76	Fair	62	"	38.60	Rain	40
3	"	76	"	58	Cloudy	48.53	Snow	36
4	Fair	80	"	62	"	38.46	Cloudy	36
5	"	76	"	58	Fair	36.50	Fair	34.42
6	"	86	"	60	"	36.46	Hazy	48.56
7	Rain	86	"	61	"	36.44	Cloudy	40
8	Cloudy	84	"	60	"	44.51	Fair	36.42
9	Rain	76	Shower	64	Rain	37	"	28
10	Cloudy	68	Fair	51	Fair	40.54	"	28
11	Fair	70	"	40	"	42.58	"	28½
12	Showers	72	"	38	Rain	62	"	27
13	Fair	76	"	40	"	50,48	"	28
14	Rain	58	"	40.50	Fair	52	"	30
15	Fair	74	"	36.38	"	54	"	18
16	"	77	"	38.58	Rain	58	"	32
17	Rain	78	Hazy	40.62	Fair	66	H'vy R'n	38
18	Fair	80	Fair	42.63	"	56.62	Snow	38
19	"	82	"	62	"	56.62	"	34
20	Rain	71	Rain	48.64	"	59.66	Fair	26
21	"	66	Fair	36.71	Rain	60	Cloudy	16
22	"	68	Rain	60.64	Showery	60.68	Rain	34
23	"	64	Fair	58	Fair	52	Snow	34
24	Fair	70	Windy	40.44	"	60	Fair	19
25	"	72	Fair	36.48	"	32.44	"	19
26	"	68	"	42.50	"	30.48	Cloudy	36
27	"	70	Rain	51.57	Cloudy	40	Fair	38
28	Cloudy	66	"	50.56	Fair	52	Cloudy	30
29	Fair	68	Ch'g'ab'e	44.55	Cloudy	42.50	Snow	28
30	Cloudy	66	Fair	44.58	"	48	"	26
31			"	44.63			"	20

N. B.—The figures in the foregoing tables were recorded from observations made at 6 o'clock A. M., during the months of December, January, February and March; and at noon during the remainder of the year. Where two columns of figures are given, the first refers to the morning, and the second to the Meridian observations.

Snow fell, according to this table, on eighteen different days, yet at no time did its depth exceed ten inches, or the ground remain covered longer than fifteen consecutive days. Out door work suffered but little interruption during this season.

Of the rain fall only partial records have been kept, and none for any successive number of years. From limited statistics on hand, and by comparison with localities in adjoining States where accurate observations were made, the average annual amount is estimated at 32 to 36 inches, which is from 7 to 10 inches less than recorded at New York. Philadelphia Washington, and Cincinnati. The distribution of rain throughout the whole State is remarkably favorable to seasonable vegetation. Total failures of crops from excess or insufficiency of humidity, are unknown in the history of the country, and droughts like those which so frequently blast the the hopes of the husbandman in the West, are out of the question under the genial atmosphereical condition of the Middle States.

Hail storms destructive to crops are of very rare occurrence, not more than two or three of very limited extent being remembered since the first settlement of the State. Tornadoes, those fearful scourges of the western plains, are scarcely known by name; ordinary high winds are materially tempered by the unevenness of the surface which affords abundant shelter to dwellings, orchards, vineyards and to herds and flocks in the open air.

The term *sultry*, in the above table, is applied to those days on which, for some time immediately before or after noon, the gentle breeze peculiar to our level is not perceptible in the wave of the foliage. This state of the atmosphere is quite unusual, and generally relieved by refreshing showers, or intervening night, after a few hours duration.

The following calendar of farming operations will, with unimportant exceptions, be found applicable to the whole Ohio valley and Lower Potomac sections of the State.

February 28. Plant early potatoes. Break up sod.

March 1. Ploughing, 10th, sow oats, timothy, blue grass, clover, set out trees and vines, sow early garden vegetables. Maple sugar manufactured. 15th, cattle turned out on blue grass.

April 1. Sow late oats and flax ; plant late potatoes. 15th. Sow main crop of garden vegetables. Cherry, plum, apple and peach trees in bloom. Poplar and maple leafing, turn cattle on timothy and clover. 25th Beans and cucumbers planted, also early corn. 31st Plant and sow all late garden vegetables, also sweet potatoes and watermelons.

May 1. Slight white frosts to be expected first week, sheep shearing, timber leafing generally, cattle turned out on woods range, plant sorghum. May 10—20, Dogwood in bloom, main crop of corn planted, pumpkins and late beans. 31st. Corn and potatoes planted on fresh cleared ground. Grapes in bloom.

June 8. Plant tobacco, new settlers still planting corn on fresh cleared land, clover in bloom. 15th, Harvesting clover, late cucumbers, beans, melons and even potatoes planted. Early grass fed cattle sent to market.

July 1, Early potatoes ripe. 15th, Sow buckwheat, rye and wheat harvest, commence cutting timothy. 25th. Oat harvest, last working of corn, early apples ripe.

August 10. Sow turnips. 15th. Finish hay harvest, plough for wheat and rye, peaches and melons ripe. 25th. Isabella, Hartford Prolific and Concord grapes maturing.

September 1—10. Cut tobacco, sow wheat, rye and timothy, Catawba and Norton's Virginia Seedling grape maturing. 15th. Cutting corn. 25th. Harvesting buckwheat.

October 1—15. First white frosts, cutting late corn, sowing wheat and rye on corn ground. Cutting sorghum and making syrup. 25th. Digging late potatoes, leaves falling fast. Late fat stock sent to market.

November 1—15. Gathering turnips and other root crops, husking corn in the field, commence winter feeding young stock and milch cows. 31st. Winter feeding generally.

THE LOWER POTOMAC COUNTIES

Morgan, Berkeley and Jefferson, scarcely require a separate chapter under the head of climate, for although located on the opposite side of the Alleghanies, with atmospherical phases varying perhaps in time and intensity from those on the western slope, the difference, as affecting healthfulness and fertility, is too unimportant to be noticed. The whole of the Potomac valley is not less remarkable for its delightful climate than for the picturesque charm of its scenery, and its bounteous share of the natural elements of wealth.

Upon the whole, the impression produced by the climate of West Virginia upon the settler from other regions, or the traveler accustomed to reason from cause to effect is that, here man has little or nothing to fear from the caprices of the elements, and the observance of the simple laws of nature cannot fail to secure health, long life, comfort and abundant pecuniary success to the industrious tiller of the soil.

But the force of this conclusion is felt by no one so keenly, as by the native West Virginian, whom the fame of the smooth and boundless prairie has allured to the realms of fever and drought, and who with a broken spirit in a shattered frame, is happy to return alive to the shady valleys and the murmuring brooks of his native land.

SURFACE AND SOIL.

The natural features of West Virginia, named at the head of this chapter, are, in a geographical and economical sense, so closely related to each other as to demand a connected consideration for the practical purposes of this manual.

To the dweller of the lowlands not familiar with mountain topography, a broken region like West Virginia, especially when viewed from a railroad train in motion, appears like an irregular, labyrinthical network of hill and dale, of mountain and valley. Yet nothing becomes more simple to the understanding than the Alleghany system, when inquiry is directed to the origin of things.

The Alleghany ridge, which extends from the St. Lawrence river in Canada, in a southwesterly direction to the Black Mountain in North Carolina, forms, in West Virginia, the watershed between the Atlantic ocean and the Mississippi valley. In the northern part of Maine this chain attains a height of 5300 feet, in New Hampshire (the White Mountains) 6620 feet, and the Black Mountain in North Carolina, 6476 feet, while in West Virginia the highest summit does not much exceed 2500 feet. There is every reason to believe, however, that its height was much greater at a distant geological period, before the summit was worn down to level of the table lands by the action of the water, and atmospheric causes. In the Alleghany and Blue Ridge system, the strata of the *mountains proper* are all inclined to a degree indicating upheaval by plutonic action, at a period prior to the abrasion of West Virginia *hills.* This action is not supposed to have been instantaneous, but slow and gradual, during two or three distinct epochs separated by intervals of comparative repose, as indicated by distinct series of upheaved strata, resting upon each other unconformably or at different degrees of inclination.

Then an immense lake or sea, whose boundaries cannot now be exactly defined, extended from the Alleghany to the Rocky mountains, fed by large rivers and occasional floods, which carried to its bed the diluvial earth and mineral detritus of an extensive surrounding continent. In this manner were successively deposited those strata of the secondary formation, which comprise not only the slates, limestones, sandstones, conglomerates, marls, coals, ores, shales, clays and sands now cropping out of the hillsides in this State, but a continuation or a repetition of the same strata to a depth—below the water level—estimated at from 40 to 50,000 feet.

How often in the course of this enormous accumulation the bed of the sea was laid dry by its own elevation, or by subsidence of surrounding levels; how long it remained above water after each elevation, and whether vegetation and animal life flourished upon its surface during those periods, it is not essential to consider for the present purpose. One great fact is self-evident; that after countless ages of gradual deposit, there finally emerged from this body of water, the dry land of which 23,000 square miles are now embraced within the State of West Virginia.

The reader not familiar with the principles of Geology, and requiring facts in support of what to him may appear a speculative theory, is referred to the sea shells, corals and other remains of aquatic life still found near the summits of our highest mountains, in the calcareous stratum of the hills in the rear of Covington, Kentucky; in Ohio near the mouth of the Little Miami river, and at various other points of the Ohio valley, all at different levels, indicating a great number of successive submersions by alluvial deposits. Equally convincing are the petrifactions and impressions of flowers, tropical ferns, stems and leaves of trees, and even fruits of extinct species, found in clays, shales, lime, sandrock and the coal seams all over the State.*

Fresh from its long submersion, the new territory probably represented an undulating plain, or basin, sloping from near the Rocky and Alleghany mountains, with intervening corrugations, towards the line of its lowest depression, now the main valley of the Mississippi river. In the process of drying, minor corrugations were undoubtedly formed, and when rain fell upon this soft, new made surface, the running waters, seeking their level, gradually washed and carved out the innumerable valleys, gulches, and drains we now behold, carrying the disintegrated soil far away into the Gulf of Mexico, and repeating, even now, at the mouth of the Mississippi, the process of sedimentary accummulation formerly accomplished at its source.

That this erosion of the valleys in West Virginia was extremely slow and gradual, is evident from the

---

*Mastodon teeth seven inches long and four inches in diameter were lately laid bare by the wash of ravines in the counties of Doddridge and Wood.

rounded shape of the hills, the almost total absence of precipices, the general prevalence and vigorous growth of timber, and the accumulation of arable soil and humus to the depth of several feet, even on hillsides inclining at an angle of 45 degrees. With the exception of the passage of the Tygart's Valley and Cheat rivers through Laurel Hill, of the New river through Cotton Hill or Gauley mountain, and the Potomac through the Blue Ridge at Harper's Ferry, there are no instances of violent action of the waters. It is even likely that these disruptions are but the effect of cataracts precipitated from the lakes formerly enclosed, and dammed by the ridges parallel to the Alleghanies, until the bed of the fall, gradually wearing backward, as in the case of Niagara falls in our days, finally gave way under the pressure. Each stream descending from the mountains forms a distinct and separate valley, taking up tributaries on its way, but never forking again in its downward course; so that the traveler ascending the hill on either side of a stream at its mouth, may reach its source by following the dividing ridge to the distant mountain, without once crossing water.

From what preceeds it may be justly inferred that hills are never out of sight in West Virginia, and occupy by far the greater portion of the surface. The proportion of alluvial or bottom land throughout the State, has been estimated at 30 per cent. In the valleys of the Ohio, the Great and Little Kanawha, the Monongahala and the Lower Potomac, as much as 50 or 60 per cent. of bottom is not an uncommon rate. On the streams next in importance the proportion varies from 10 to 30 and 40 per cent. while at the headwaters of the tributaries the bottom is often confined to a few yards in width, with lower summits and gentler slopes by way of compensation. As a general rule, the width of the valley is proportioned to the size of the stream, yet there are numerous exceptions; narrow valleys being found for miles at a stretch along good sized rivers, while many small creeks afford here and there quite extensive bottoms. Much depends in this respect upon the nature of the strata in the adjoining hills; soft material being more easily disintegrated, furnishes wider valleys and gentler slopes. An experienced eye will therefore readily judge of the nature of the soil by the shape and height of the hills.

Notwithstanding the systematic—almost monotonous character of West Virginia topography, the varied charm and splendor of her scenery are not less celebrated than her delightful climate. Abler pens have done justice to the subject, and from their pictures a few of the most characteristic scenes are selected:

"Now mount your nag and be off! As you descend the mountain path faintly discerned before you, and breathe the pure fresh air of the hills, cast your eyes upon the most impressive scenes, for Nature is there in all her glory. Far down, in the valley to the right, winds a a lovely stream; there hid by the foliage overarching its bright waters—anon it appears in a clearing—again, concealed by a sweep of the mountain you are descending—still beyond, it seems diminished to a silvery thread. To the right and front is a huge mountain in luxuriant verdure, at places curving far into the plain, and at those points, and at the summits, bathed in a sea of golden light, at others receding, thrown into dark, sombre, forbidding shades. Beyond are mountains piled on mountains, like an uptossed sea of ridges, until they melt away in the distance, and imagination fancies others still farther on. High in blue ether float yon clouds of snowy white, and far above them, in majestic flight, sails the bird of the mountain, with an air as wild, as free as the spirit of liberty. How every thing is rejoicing all around! Innumerable songsters are warbling sweetest music; those wild flowers, with scarce the morning dew from off their lips, are opening their bright cheeks to the sun; and even the tiny insects flitting through the air, join in the universal hallalujah! Now fast losing the scene, you are entering the dark, solemn forest, densely matted above with vines, almost excluding the light of day. You are soon at the base of the mountains, and from the copse before you out starts a deer! The graceful animal pricks up its ears, distends its nostrils in fear, and, gathering its slender limbs ready for a spring, then bounds away, ever hillocks and through ravines, and is seen no more. The stream, broad and shallow, is winding its way across your road with gentle murmurings—splash! splash! goes your horse's feet into the water; forty times in ten miles does it cross your road, and in various places for many hundred yards your course is directly through it. There are no bridges upon it, there are comparatively few in Western Virginia.

[*Howe's Hy. & Ant. of Virginia*, 1846.

"The scenery of West Virginia is worthy of a volume, rather than the fragment of a chapter. Under the influence of so genial a climate, that semitropical forms of vegetation are almost native of its soil, its flora may safely be presumed to equal, if not to surpass, in variety and magnificence, the wealth of any other State or Continent. In its fauna it is equally distiguished. Birds, beautiful in plumage and sweet in song, give life, and grace and cheerfulness to field and forest. The surface is infinite variety, rills meet in rivulets and rivulets swiftly swell into rivers, which leap their mountain barriers and quietly subside into the placidity of the plains below. Mountains rise like little Alps on Alps; glades, those meadows of the mountain, freshen the summer atmosphere with delicious coldness; cultivated slopes, as in Greenbrier and other of the older counties, move the imagination, as by a wand of enchantment; deep, winding, fertile valleys, lie at the foot of beettling bluffs, full of fatness of fertility. Everywhere the vision is greeted with variety and beauty. Nature has not only been partial, but prodigal; yet the hand of man is needed to direct and to use this benificence of benefaction.

European travelers have been enraptured with the ever varying scenery of the Cheat river region, as seen in a trip by rail; and none have been more impressed by it than those who have climbed the Alps, and viewed with awe their towering heights and darkening depths beneath. It exerts unwonted emotions thus to wind around the steep side of a mountain spur, and emerge from its shadows into a sunlit slope that falls abruptly away, at the very edge of the car, hundreds of feet, and reveals at the bottom a long and winding valley, a singularly dark stream, whose chocolate colored waters contrast, while harmonizing with the forest growth that reaches from the golden sunlight of the mountain top down to the river's brink. * * * The sturdiness of the forests, the hardy vigor of all vegetable life, the munificence of all visible nature, impress the traveler accustomed to see bare rock and stinted vegetation amid mountain scenery. There is nothing of poverty suggested, and no intimation of sterility; few jutting crags are seen, unless hewn out of the mountain side in cutting the wild pathway of the railroad; and no rough rocks, piled heap upon heap, offend the eye as it sweeps the gracefully rounded knobs. * * * Lonely as the vast reaches of woodland appear, and bold and varied as is the contour of the mountain face, there is always present the suggestion that every acre is habitable—that the hand of art may heighten the beauties and soften the few asperities of the scene.

The traveler pursues his westward way down the Alleghanian slope, through scenery similar in its type, but slowly and continually modifying, till it becomes noticeable only as a hilly, fruitful country, divided into farms naturally suited to the diverse uses of meadows, pasturage, and tillage, and watered with frequent and rapid streams.

In the eastern section of the State, the lower Shenandoah valley presents views of greater beauty, with less of wildness and grandeur. More than a hundred miles, between Harper's Ferry and Cumberland, the Potomac, "a flashing thread of silver," runs out a winding boundary between Maryland and West Virginia; and the neighboring meadows, and wheat fields and golden fruited orchards, and wild forests, make graceful pictures of rural realities and possibilities that touch the heart while they delight the eye.

The scenery of West Virginia is worthy of the highest efforts of the painter and the poet. The "Hawk's Nest" mountain, a thousand feet in almost perpendicular height; its "Hanging Rocks" leaning over the perpendicular, like the tower of Pisa, five hundred feet from the surface; its "Lost River" burrowing in the earth, and "revisiting the glimpses of the moon" in numerous outlets far away; its caves and falls, and Indian mounds; these, and many other peculiar features of her landscape, are worthy of more accurate delineation. 'This scenery," said the historian Bancroft, a few years ago, "has a character of grandeur of its own; and in the wonderful varieties of forest and lawn, of river and mountain, of nature in her savage wildness and nature in her loveliest forms, presents a series of pictures which no well educated American should leave unvisited. We cross the Atlantic in quest of attractive scenes; and lo! we have at home, alongside of the great central iron pathway, views that excel anything that can be seen among the mountains of Scotland, or in the passes of the Appennines;" and had the writer visited the beautiful valley of the Great Kanawha, his rapture, with no danger of abatement, might have warmed into a still brighter glow.

[*Dodge's West Virginia.*

The total absence of waste and sterile areas, that all pervading freshness and vigor of vegetation, alluded to in the above extracts, obtrude themselves to the tourist no less than to the practical economist. Among the mineral strata edging out of the West Virginia hills, there are absolutely none in which analysis does not recognize superior elements of fertility. The prevailing ingredients of our soils are silica, alumina, or pure clay, marl, lime, magnesia and iron, which the very unevenness of the surface tends to amalgamate to the greatest practical advantage. Thus the alluvial or bottom lands, composed of the diluvium from adjacent and distant hills, combine mechanically and chemically every kind of mineral and vegetable decomposition in the country. This soil, which varies in depth from 2 to 30 or 40 feet produces the largest timber and the rankest crops, and resting upon a substantial basis of dark loam and fertile clay, exceeds in reliability and endurance the black, rich but thirsty and chaffy soils of the western prairies.

The second bottom, or first bench, is generally representative of the rocks prevailing upon this level, with a strong admixture of the strata above, brought down by the gradual slips and the wash of rains, and accumulated probably to a great extent before the present vegetation took possession of the surface. Ascending, we find the soil gradually less mixed in substance and color; the timber is less varied and on steeper planes less thrifty. When the top of the ridge is sharp and narrow, the bare rock is found but a few inches below and not seldom protruding above the surface, but when flat or but gently inclined, as in a majority of cases, we find a deep, arable soil, heavily coated with humus and producing, with few exceptions, the identical timber and crops found in the alluvial valley below. Some of the most comfortable rural homesteads, surrounded by orchards, gardens and meadows, and supplied with never-failing springs are found upon the tops of hills from 150 to 300 feet above the valleys.

Extensive flats on the summits are the exception in that larger portion of West Virginia, which, viewed from a prominence, resembles a sea of billowy hills; but they entirely absorb the scene in the table lands referred to in the chapter on climate. Here undulating plains, which but for their majestic timber would recall to mind an Illinois prairie, reach along the mountain summits for miles in length and breadth, with scarcely here and there a swell sufficiently bold to divide the waters. Although less favored than the residue of the State in the sum of temperature, these mountain plains would have been the earliest settled and improved, had they been equally accessible from the natural highways. Even in their present relative seclusion, their charm upon the beholder is almost irresistible, and it requires a serious effort of reason over inclination to withstand the temptation of settlement in the face of prevailing inconveniences.

Not only the smoothness of the surface, the pure air and water, and the charm of the landscape, but also the depth and quality of the soil, mostly a rich, calcarous loam, class these table lands among the most intrinsically valuable in the State. The luxuriant meadows and grazing ranges of Greenbrier and Monroe counties exhibit the capacity of such lands in the state of improvement, while their native splendor is nowhere more impressive than at the headwaters of the Cheat and Greenbrier rivers, in the adjoining extremities of Randolph, Pocahontas and Pendleton counties.

A peculiarity, worthy of notice in these regions, is that the timber, though of unsurpassed growth and vigor, does not include poplar, hickory or oak, while gigantic specimens of wild cherry and black walnut are abundantly scattered among the representatives of beech, maple, ash, birch, hemlock and spruce. Again, the undergrowth which obstructs the view and increases the labor of clearing in the lower sections, is almost totally absent here, and does not even make its appearance after the clearing or girdling of the timber lets in the heat and light of the sun.

The depth of the soil on the hillsides throughout the State varies from 1 to 10 feet or more, in proportion to the inclination of the surface, or character of the rock beneath, yet subject to modifications, induced by difference of exposure. Thus the southern and southwestern slopes directly facing the sun's rays at the time of their greatest intensity, and the winds and rains prevailing from that quarter, exhibit a more shallow soil, generally of the clay variety, denuded of the lighter vegetable coating, and inclined to produce more brushwood than heavy timber. The opposite and more sheltered exposures retaining all the vegetable matter decaying on their surface, are but little inferior to the bottom lands in enduring fertility; and after being cultivated in grain during a number of years, from the base to the very summit of the hills, are converted into luxuriant pastures and meadows.

It is a matter of general remark and frequent surprise, that crops growing on our hillsides do not seem to be affected by the dryness of the soil, which is presumed to increase with elevation. The reason of this is very simple. The strata of rock, coal and earth of which our hills are composed being all deposited horizontally, or nearly so, the rain water, filtering through the earth and the fissures in the rocks and seeking its level, gradually finds its way to the surface again between the looser seams, and slowly but constantly dripping, so long as the supply lasts within, spreads and distributes fertilizing humidity over the whole surface of the slope. Whenever the descending water is obstructed in its progress by a stratum of impermeable clay or unfissured sand rock, numerous and copious springs on the sloping surface are the result.

It is also owing to this horizontal stratification that almost every section of the State outside of the mountain region proper, exhibits, though in different relative proportions, the soil and mineral strata of every other section, In some counties limestone may predominate, and sandrock in others; yet without any material difference in their respective agricultural productions, while nearly throughout the whole State may be noticed at different levels, those rich, dark, crumbling shales so welcome to the eye of the practical judge of agricultural soil.

It may be assumed in conclusion, that there are no large scopes of virgin soil in West Virginia not liable to be rendered perfectly friable and productive under proper mechanical treatment, without the use of manure, and that the average fertilty of the State ranks at least equal with that of any of the surrounding States. Even if agricultural statistics were entirely reliable as datas for comparison, the result would show quite favorably for West Virginia; but it is evident to all who have observed the imperfect and slovenly style of cultivation prevailing here, that the actual or estimated production is far below the true producing capacity of the country.

AGRICULTURE.

From the subject of soil we are at once led into the consideration of agricultural production, and it is to explain in part why a hilly region like West Virginia lays claim to farming capacity, that so much space was devoted to the description of her surface and soil.

When in this capacity, West Virginia is brought into comparison with prairie States like Indiana, Iowa or Illinois, where fields of miles in extent offer no obstruction to the use of the most perfect farming machinery, the result in bushels per acre is not expected to be in her favor. But until the census of of 1870 settles this question with accuracy, it is by no means difficult to show that West Virginia—all other things being equal—produces the largest value on any given area, and consequently, that whatever farming is done here, yields a larger return upon the capital and labor invested than it would in the West. The difference is attributable to the simple fact that the market of West Virginia products is right at home, or distant at farthest but one days transportation from the source of production, while the crops of the West have to seek their market over land and sea, hundreds or thousands of miles away.

No statistical report of agriculture in West Virginia having been made since her advent among the States, we can, for comparison between her production and that of other States, only approximate results in support of this proposition, by calculating the value of western crops at West Virginia prices. Thus, Illinois produced in 1866, as per statistical report of United States Department of Agriculture:

Indian Corn, bush.	155,844,350	at $0.43	$67,013,070
Wheat "	28,551,421	" 1.93	55,104,243
Rye "	666,455	" 79	526,500
Oats "	30,054,370	" 33	9,917,942
Barley "	1,037,763	" 68	705,672
Buckwheat "	273,010	" 1.07	292,121
Potatoes "	5,102.085	" 64	3,265,302
Tobacco, pds.	17,556,981	" 9¾	1,631,470
Hay, tons	2,340,063	" 9.27	21,692,284
Total			$160,148,704

During the same year the average prices in West Virginia of the products above enumerated were as follows:

Indian corn, (per bushel) 75c; wheat $2; rye $1; Oats 50c; Barley $1.25; Buckwheat $1.25; Potatoes 75c; Tobacco, (per pound) 12c; Hay, (per ton) $10. At these rates the total product of Illinois would be $211,-821,155. Difference in favor of West Virginia prices $57,-692,457, or 32 per cent.

The official report from which the above was taken, gives the total number of acres cultivated in each crop, in Illinois, and also the production of each, per acre, as follows:

Indian corn	31.6	Buckwheat	16.8
Wheat	10 .	Potatoes	86.5
Rye	15.6	Tobacco, (pds)	686.
Oats	34	Hay, (tons)	1.47
Barley	25		

This estimate, we must admit, strikes us somewhat moderate for Illinois, especially in regard to the articles of corn and hay, though no one acquainted with *our* average production will regard it as too high for West Virginia; except perhaps for wheat, a crop which, owing to the practice of late sowing, after gathering the corn crop, does not furnish a yield commensurate with the true capacity of the soil.

INDIAN CORN.

Old inhabitants of the Ohio valley remember the time when crops of 100 to 120 bushels of Indian corn per acre were not unusual there. Only a few years ago the premium at the Ohio County Agricultural Fair was awarded to a crop of 144 bushels per acre in Marshall county. The bottoms cleared 60 or 70 years ago, and subject to overflowing once in 15 or 20 years, are still producing from 60 to 80 bushels per acre, on an average. The same applies to the bottom land of any river or creek, however small, in the State, when cultivated with moderate care and neatness. The same return is not unfrequently obtained on hillsides and ridges in favorable exposures, for several years after clearing, and again after having been sodded and grazed a few years, without any other manuring than the droppings of the running stock, and so on in rotation, without any perceptible diminution of yield.

In the prairie States, excessive droughts and sweeping tornadoes, grasshoppers, &c., may contribute materially to reduce the crop of Indian corn to an average of 32 bushels per acre, but in West Virginia this figure would be largely exceeded but for the circumstance, that a large portion of each years crop is raised on fresh cleared ground, obstructed by roots and stumps, and exposed to the depredations of vermin from the adjacent forest.

The total yield of Indian corn in 1860 is given as 7,858,647 bushels. Nearly all of this crop is generally consumed within the State, and none exported, except after conversion into fat beef or pork. It costs so little here to rear live stock up to fattening age, on the woodspasture and beech, acorn and chestnut mast still abounding in the interior, that the operation of fattening is comparatively cheap, and animals in marketable condition are bought away from the producers door for ready cash without further trouble or expense. In addition to these advantages, a large portion of the grain so invested returns to the soil in the shape of manure. Exporting grain would impoverish the farm; feeding to live stock enriches it. Necessity, in the shape of bad roads, has taught West Virginians the virtue of this golden rule.

Whatever corn is not used in that way or for household purposes, finds a ready market in the vicinity of its production at the hands of new settlers or in the nearest towns. Corn is cash at all times. During the last ten years the price has never fallen below 60 or 75 cents near the Ohio river, and frequently ranged from $1.25 to $1.50 in the interior.

Indian corn is the first and main reliance of the new settler on a woodland farm, and seldom or never deceives his expectations. There has not been a *total* failure of this crop since the first settlement of the State. The writer remembers of no *partial* failure worth mentioning during the 25 years of his residence. On five or six acres of fresh cleared land, of which four-fifths are planted in corn, pumpkins and beans, and the rest in potatoes, sorghum, and garden vegetables, an average sized pioneer family can subsist without stint during the first year, besides keeping a cow and calf, wintering a horse and fattening a couple of respectable porkers. No long feed is required but the cornfodder, stalk and all, which, when properly cured and fed without waste, will carry the stock through the winter in good living order.

WHEAT.

The production of this grain in West Virginia is given in the Census of 1860 at 2,302,567 bushels, or a fraction over six bushels to the inhabitant. This would be inadequate to the home consumption, were it not for the partial use of corn, rye and buckwheat bread, especially in the more remote and recently settled counties.

In estimating the actual average yield of wheat at 10 bushels per acre, it is not intended to fix the producing capacity at so low a figure. This capacity cannot be accurately determined in the present imperfect state of agriculture in the State. By reference to the table of production by counties, at the end of this chapter, it will be seen that the oldest and more accessible counties are by far the largest producers, not only because their area devoted to wheat is greater, but also the soil and surface are in a better condition for thorough cultivation, and some respect is paid to the principles of rotation. There being an abundance of open land on old farms, preparation can be made in due season; seeding is done in August, or early in September, and the crop maturing early in consequence, is less subject to accidents of weather. The harvesting and thrashing are done in the most economical style, crops of 15 bushels per acre, on average soil, or of 20 to 25 bushels on limestone land are therefore by no means unusual. Crops of 30 bushels are frequently obtained in Harrison, Barbour and Upshur, and one of 40 bushels per acre is reported from Marshall county.

On the other hand, in the newer sections, where, as before mentioned, cleared land is less abundant, and wheat is sown late after the corn is cut, among stumps and roots, the ploughing performed with a one horse shovel, without harrowing or rolling, most of the seed falls either too deep or too shallow for vegetation. Coming up late, the crop is liable to be further diminished by hard, dry frosts; late ripening exposes it to rust, wevil and other accidents; and the harvesting being done by hand, and the thrashing by flail, or the horses hoof, more or less waste is inevitable. Frequently wheat is slovenly sown in rough new land, along with timothy, principally to protect the young grass against the effect of frost and heat. Under these circumstances, a crop of more than 6 or 8 bushels per acre would surpass expectations. Yet this same land when broken up again after a few years, will, under proper cultivation, readily yield twice or three times that amount.

Most of the known varieties of winter wheat have been introduced and experimented with in this State, with more or less success, according to soil and season, the white, flinty smooth, and early bearded varieties proving the most reliable. Spring wheat is yielding but moderate returns so far as tried, and is not gaining much favor.

RYE.

This crop is not very generally cultivated as yet, for the reason, probably, that it requires the same season, the same labor and care as wheat, without being quite so profitable and necessary. Rye bread is not much used where corn abounds, and for distilling purposes, there is little or no market near. In the luxuriance of its growth, rye far exceeds other small grain in the State; often attaining a height of 5 to 7 feet. It is much less sensitive to quality of soil, to frost and indifferent cultivation, for which reason rye is frequently sown with good results in new cleared land which did not get ready for the plough in spring, or in rough patches too steep for the cultivation of corn. Rye is upon the average a safe and reliable crop, and adapted to almost any kind of soil in the State, though thriving best on rich sandy loam.

OATS.

With reasonable and careful cultivation oats must always be a profitable crop in West Virginia, being liable to no accidents, except a touch of rust in persistent July showers, which rarely occur. The largest crops of this grain are produced in the counties nearest market or transportation, or in the mountains and glades where the conditions of climate, unpropitious to Indian corn, are favorable to oats. Upon those higher levels, the grain is remarkable for its fullness and weight, and not disposed to lodge as in alluvial soil. The production per acre ranges between 30 and 40 bushels and crops of 50 and 60 bushels per acre have been obtained under favorable circumstances.

BARLEY.

In the absence of convenient markets, the cultivation of barley has not received much attention up to date. Of 41,373 bushels (not 60,368 as officially misprinted), 38,000 were produced by the river counties of Hancock, Brooke, Ohio and Marshall, which find ready sale at the breweries of the city of Wheeling, and at other points on the upper Ohio. Like oats, it flourishes well in almost any soil, provided it be light and well drained. Its average production is reported at 25 bushels per acre, which at the current price of $1.25 per bushel is highly encouraging.

BUCKWHEAT.

This popular cereal thrives with little or no care in every part of the State, and is cultivated most extensively in the upper Ohio river and mountain counties. Preston county alone produces 95,357 bushels, or one-fourth of the entire crop of the State. This indicates its peculiar adaptedness to the colder sections, the glades and table lands, where it constitutes a household article of almost primary necessity. Indeed, in the skillful hands of the local matrons, it attains the rank of a culinary luxury second to none in the Alleghany regions. Buckwheat cakes are baked and eaten almost everywhere, and as soon forgotten, but buckwheat cakes with Glade butter, mountain honey or maple syrup, are imperishably linked in the memory of the traveler with the savory venison steak, or the luscious trout, all of which are commonly found together on the hospitable board of every industrious mountaineer.

The yield of this grain is extremely variable in different soils. The writer has recorded one crop in one of the central counties of 22 bushels from 3½ pecks of seed, surface not measured, and another of 54 bushels per acre. The largest yields are obtained in good dry loam, especially when sod has been ploughed under. In rich alluvial the growth is inclined to go to straw, which induces lodging before maturity.

In the mountains, buckwheat is sown much earlier than elsewhere, in order to escape fall frosts which are fatal to it. In the lower counties the middle of July is early enough for seeding, and if desired, two crops may be obtained from the same field, provided the first be sown early in April. The last crop is generally the heaviest, being less exposed to blight from heat. To the new settler this rapidity of growth is of valuable assistance as it enables him to take a crop from the land cleaned up too late for corn, without waiting for returns until the following summer, as in the case of wheat and rye.

Owing to the shade which thickly sowed buckwheat affords to the earth, it is of superior efficiency in extirpating the rank weeds which generally take possession of fresh cleared ground.

THE POTATO.

This tuber is not cultivated beyond the demands of home consumption, except in the sections most convenient to market. Marshall, Preston, Hampshire, Wood and Jackson take the lead, the first named with a production of 44,944 bushels in 1860. Baltimore, Cincinnati, Louisville and other river points as far down as New Orleans, afford the most accessible and profitable markets.

Potatoes are grown successfully in every part of the State, and yield the largest crops in deep loams, moderately dry, or in any friable calcareous soil, no matter whether on low ground or upland. In the Glades and table land regions, especially in fresh turned sod, they are reputed to be remarkably mealy, well flavored, and less exposed to disease that in the valleys. The potato rot which has proved so destructive elsewhere, never yet obtained a fair hold in West Virginia, and made its appearance only to a limited extent once or twice in twenty years in some of the older counties, when barnyard manure had been used in planting. On fresh cleared, gentle slopes, no crop is more remunerative. When planted in hills 3 to 3½ feet apart each way, or in drills the same distance apart from 150 to 250 bushels may be raised per acre; and judging from experiments on small patches, even larger yields may be expected under neat and thorough cultivation.

In the interior counties, where the wants of new settlers for food and seed sustain a constant demand, the price ranges from 75 cts. to $1, and even $1.25 per bushel. But in the river counties where the products of Ohio and Pennsylvania compete with ours, potatoes fall frequently as low as 40 to 50 cents per bushel. Yet even these rates, owing to the large yield per acre, the crop is highly profitable, and its cultivation largely increasing.

In former times the Baltimore Blues, Pinkeye, Meshannock, Mercer and Long John or Stock potato, were universal favorites, and are still popular, though of late years some new varieties, the Peach Blow among the rest, were introduced with great success. This variety yields well in most soils, except moist alluvial, where, unless the draining is perfect, it suffers from wet rot.

The sweet potato, (Convolvus batatas) is well adapted to the climate and remarkably productive in its favorite element—a rich sandy loam—or black fresh cleared land, well stirred. Prices range from $1 to 1.50 in the fall, and even $2 per bushel early in the season.

THE TURNIP.

This is another product of great value to the new settler, because like buckwheat and rye, though with less labor, it may be raised on any virgin soil not sufficiently cleared for corn. Indeed, it is in the new, untilled ground, yet covered with the ashes of the burned timber, that the turnip matures most rapidly, and without further labor, attains the highest degree of succulence and nutritiveness. The seed is sown upon the surface, roughly prepared with the bulltongue or one horse shovel, and harrowed in with a large bundle of limbs or brush. When the seeding is done evenly and not too thickly, so that not more than three or four plants will grow upon one square yard, from two to four hundred bushels may be obtained per acre. When cut up with straw or corn fodder, turnips will take milch cows through the winter in good condition, with little or no grain, and it is only on account of the trouble required by this preparation, that this crop is not more extensively cultivated by our native, easy going farmers.

The flat English, or sweet white turnip is the most generally used and profitable here, Rutabaga or Swedish Turnips receiving as yet but little attention. In old land, except fresh turned sod, the product is apt to be less thrifty and tender, and more exposed to insects and drought. Manuring adds to the volume, but not to the quality of the crop. New land is therefore always preferred here when at hand.

HAY.

In a State so largely devoted to stock farming as West Virginia, the hay crop is an object of primary importance, as it determines the capacity of the country for the breeding and permanent improvement of stock. Many sections of the continent are unsurpassed for range or summer grazing, but unsuited for maturing and propagating stock. In West Virginia, climate, soil, water, grass and grain are in the highest degree favorable to stock farming as a business, complete in all its branches, and susceptible of every improvement elsewhere attained.

The hay crop of 1860 is officially given at 156,136 tuns of 2000 pounds, or only 2-5 of a tun for every horse, ass, mule, milk cow and head of other horned cattle in the State, except sheep. As this is only about one-half of the average quantity of dry forage required in our climate, per head, it may be assumed that the other half is supplied by corn fodder and other straw, and by winter pasture not grazed short in the fall. At the very low estimate of 1⅓ tuns to the acre, it would appear, that only one acre in twenty-three of the improved land in the State is cropped in hay, which common observation shows to be far below the reality. It is therefore manifest that here, as in the case of several other items, the official reports are in error, owing chiefly to the fact that many of our farmers, suspecting the assessor behind the census man, are too cautious in giving in their property.

By far the greatest proportion of West Virginia hay consists of Timothy, or Meadow Cat's Tail (*Phleum Pratense*) which, in favorable soil, attains a height of 3½ to 4 feet, and yields from is 2 to 2½ tuns per acre. Meadows in which timothy is measurably mixed with blue grass, produce less in bulk and weight, though the difference is probably compensated by fragrance and strength. Clover is not raised for hay, except in the Potomac Valley and some of the older western counties, where it enters into the rotation of crops. On the fresh soil of the newer counties, the rank growth causes clover to fall before maturity, and moreover, its curing, during the showery weather in early June, is somewhat precarious and interferes with the working of corn.

Other varieties of grasses for hay have formerly been introduced and tried, but none ever succeeded in acquiring the preference over blue grass and timothy. Among the native grasses which in course of time creep into meadows, are the red top, and a similar looking variety of blue grass, (not Kentucky) both of which, though valuable in pastures, are not profitable in meadows, as they are light in growth, and dead ripe and worthless before timothy is fit for harvest.

Timothy meadows generally occupy the smoothest and best lands on the farm, in most cases the bottoms; but heavy crops are also cut on rich hillsides, not too steep for the scythe. In the mountains, hay is cropped from every variety of surface, and blue grass being of spontaneous growth, especially on limestone land, timothy is less frequently met with. In the most improved and accessible sections, mowing machines have been in use for many years.

Unless prepared to import fertilizers, the West Virginia farmer should never export hay, as it is through the feeding of this forage in the barnyard or in the open fields, that he can mainly expect to return some substance to the soil. Yet more or less hay is continually sold for consumption in towns, and even shipped East or South when prices are inviting. The price along the Ohio river and railroad varies from $12 to 18 per ton.

Timothy, or blue grass hay requires from one to one and one-half days to cure in fair weather. It is generally put up in stacks of from two to two and a half tuns each, of which so much is from time to time hauled to the barn, as may be needed for horses, workoxen and milk cows, the balance being fed out to the stock cattle in open air.

Although upon principles of theoretical science, the simple feeding of a *portion* of the hay crop upon the field of its production, should in due course of time impoverish the land and reduce the yield, yet such a result is not verified by practical experience here. As a rule, the contrary is the case. When, in the course of from eight to twelve years, a meadow becomes moss-bound or infected with weeds and unprofitable grasses, it is broken up as deeply as possible, one or two heavy crops of corn are taken from it, after which the field is seeded down in wheat with timothy, and so soon as the grass has taken a fair start—after one or two years—the yield of hay is as *heavy as ever*. This experience is common all over the State and defies every scientific refutation.

TOBACCO.

Twenty years ago, when slavery still prevailed in Virginia, this plant, which requires a large amount of manual labor, was much more of a staple than at present. The production of the counties now comprising the new State, is given for 1860 at 2,180,316 pounds which, however, is thought considerably below the facts. Of this amount the counties of Putnam, Kanawha and Fayette, in the Kanawha Valley, and the counties of Wood, Mercer and Monroe furnished the two-thirds. Since then, circumstances consequent upon the late war have tended to decrease the cultivation, and to shift it to some extent from some of the older counties to the others more recently improved, though the Kanawha region probably still retains the lead.

West Virginia being immediately adjacent to Maryland, Virginia and Kentucky, whose products outrank all others in the Union, may be regarded as equally favorable in point of soil and climate, and it is only in skill and experience that her planters appear to be somewhat in arrear of the neighboring States.

Here it is not necessary to start the plants in hot beds as is the case farther North, but by sowing about the middle of March, on a clean, well prepared patch of ground, upon which a pile of brush was previously burned, a fine, hardy plant is obtained for transplanting on or before the 1st of June. An occasional application of soot or rich liquid manure will stimulate the growth, so as to bring the plant quickly beyond the reach of the fly.

On new land, rich in natural fertilizers, or assisted by the ashes of timber burnt upon its surface, tobacco is always a reliable and profitable crop, and even on steep hillsides seldom suffers from drought. Owing to its great value in small bulk, transportation to market is not a serious obstacle, even from the remotest sections. Under indifferent cultivation, the yield per acre varies from 800 to 1000 pounds, and under most favorable circumstances crops of 1800 and 2000 pounds have been realized.

Fresh from the field, West Virginia tobacco is probably scarcely inferior to good Kentucky, but it is in the process of drying and coloring that the skill of our planters appears to be deficient, which amounts to a difference in market value of from 16 to 20 per cent. West Virginia tobacco is now quoted in the Cincinnati and Baltimore markets at from 11 to 16 cents.

To a pioneer family commanding more force than is required to clear land for the necessary cereal and forage crops, a few acres in tobacco will prove a valuable cash resource in the start. But as the very best of soils are inevitably exhausted by successive crops, without the application of specific manures, tobacco is not to be recommended on old farms, except on fresh turned sod after several years of rest. The most fertile regions of Maryland and Virginia have been impoverished by excessive crops, and are now offered for sale in small parcels and at *seemingly* low prices to foreign emigrants, not familiar with the agricultural history of the country. The purchasers, not able to devote a small fortune to the purchase of manures, will find such lands a hard bargain, and rather than expose West Virginia to a similar condition, it would be better if never a stalk of tobacco were planted upon her soil.

SORGHUM, OR CHINESE SUGAR CANE

was first introduced into the State in 1857, and in less than three years became domesticated on almost every farm. Up to date its cultivation was confined to the production of syrup, for home consumption, but will undoubtedly assume extensive proportions, once the art of granulation or chrystallization is more generally understood. Very good samples of sugar have been produced in various sections, in some instances accidentally.

In good soil the cane attains a height of from twelve to fifteen feet, and when well matured, yield from two to three hundred gallons of syrup per acre. The Chinese black seed variety yields the largest amount, and the African Imphee, red seed, the best quality. Its gravity is generally from 9 to 10° Beaume'. The method of planting best adapted to the soil and climate is in hills, slightly closer than corn, with about four or five stalks to the hill. In this latitude the cane should be worked up as soon as possible after cutting, and if not convenient immediately, it should be stored away in small bundles accessible to free circulation of air.

MAPLE SUGAR.

In the forests of West Virginia are found at least two varieties of the Maple from which sugar is manufactured: 1st, The Sugar, Rock or Hard Maple (*Acer Saccharinum*) and the Black Maple, (*Acer nigrum*), the latter being commonly designated as Maple, simply, while the other is popularly called Sugar or Sugartree, it being also the most abundant, the richest in saccharine juice, and the most extensively developed. Both varieties flourish more or less abundantly all over the State, in the lowlands as well as in the mountains and table lands, in good soil and favorable exposures.

The production of Maple sugar for 1850 is stated at 667,178 pounds, and of syrup 71,425 gallons; which gives but a feeble idea of the producing capacity of the State. There are millions of acres of wild land on which never a tree has been tapped, and thousands of productive trees in the sugar orchards of old improved farms stand neglected for the want of time or labor to save the crop. In the lower or valley portion of the State the development is principally confined to the new settlements convenient to the timber. But in the mountain counties, where the sugar maple thrives in all its glory, in groups and groves, accidentally scattered over the sloping green as if by the tasteful hand of art, sugar making forms an important branch of husbandry or industry in the most improved neighborhoods. There also, spring coming on a litle latter, this operation does not interfere with the early work on the farm, and the favorable period of cool, frosty nights with bright sunny days, is considerably longer than in the lower warmer sections. Sugar making in the mountains is a source not only of pleasure and recreation, but of considerable profit. In the production of 1860, Greenbrier figures with 72,650 pounds; Pocahontas 63,-725; Pendleton 59,590; Monroe 46,617; Randolph 43,-692; Hardy 37,653; Monongalia 32,608; Mercer 21,009; Marion 19,520. But the writer has reason to think the figures largely under estimated, to judge from the case of Doddridge county, his former residence, whose product is stated at only 1623 pounds, while to his personal knowledge, the amount sold at the stores exceeded 2500, and probably an equal amount was retained for household use.

Among the least populated counties, Randolph, Upshur, Webster and Nicholas offer perhaps the most extensive facilities for the cheap production of maple sugar. On thousands of acres in this section, the sugartree comprises nearly one-half of the timber, and the price of land is at present so low, that the sugar crop of one year on a small portion of a tract, will pay the purchase money for the whole.

Until now, the process and contrivances used in the manufacture of maple sugar were of the most primitive order. Trees from 15 to 20 inches in diameter are selected and tapped, the incision being made in the form of a V, in which spouts of elder or sumach are inserted. Troughs to catch the sap, are split out from poplar, or other soft wood. According to the size of the "sugar camp" one or more one horse sled or ox teams, are employed to gather the sap in barrels, and haul it to the fire, which is built between two large logs, the kettles resting on these, or being suspended on a strong pole supported by rude forks. In old, permanent camps, the two logs are, in rare instances, replaced by a hearth or kiln of rude stone or brick, dispensing with the pole and forks. This is all that is required in the way of preparation; but the skill which presides at the kettles and superintends the boiling, skimming, clarifying and straining is equal to any in more advanced regions, as West Virginia maple sugar is equal to the best produced elsewhere, in flavor and appearance.

The yield per tree varies from 6 to 10 gallons per day in favorable weather, giving from ¾ to 1¼ pounds of hard sugar, besides a quantity of clear luscious syrup. This result may be realized from the same trees upon an average for 25 or 50 days in a season, and even exceeded in favorable seasons. Trees standing well apart in open fields, clear from brush and shade, yield the sweetest sap, and the largest quantity.

Well conditioned maple sugar always brings at the country stores the price of unrefined or brown New Orleans sugar. At the present price of 15 or 16 cents per pound, the product of two or three trees per acre, will pay twice for the best wild land in the mountains, in one season. This consideration alone, aside from other inducements, should stimulate the settlement of the maple regions by emigrants of limited means. Excepting the teams—and even these are often dispensed with by families blessed with a large home force—no capital is required for the manufacture of maple sugar, which is *always* a certain crop, representing a large value in a small bulk, easy of transportation, and never lacking a remunerative market.

THE DAIRY.

After all that has been said in preceeding chapters in regard to climate, soil and water, it is scarcely necessary to demonstrate at length the special adaptedness of the State to the production of milk, butter and cheese. The capacity of West Virginia under this head is only limited by her want of labor and of rapid transportation. Her butter, especially that produced in the mountains and glades, commands a higher price in the Baltimore market than the product of any other section or State. There is no reason why this should not be, and whatever skill and conveniences may yet be wanting for the more perfect manufacture and preservation of butter, will certainly be forthcoming, so soon as transportation facilities encourage production on a larger scale. From the peculiarly favored location of the State near the most populous markets on the continent, the prospects of her dairy interests are almost incalculable.

The production of butter amounted to 4,760,779 in 1860, when it exceeded that of eleven other States, but has largely increased since under the stimulus of higher prices. During the seasons most favorable to the shipment of butter, country stores seldom pay less than 20 or 30 cents per pound. In the markets of Parkersburg, Wheeling, Grafton and Charleston the retail prices vary between 40 and 60 cents from September to May. Sweet milk sells in these places at from eight to ten cents per quart and is not abundantly supplied.

In the manufacture of cheese, the State is still farther in arrear of her natural facilities, her production of 150,000 pounds being far from adequate to the home demand. Even this amount is very indifferently manufactured, altogether in a domestic way, chiefly from skimmed milk and not fit for distant markets. In comparison with the most renowned cheese producing sections of Europe, West Virginia possesses superior advantages, particularly in the cool temperature, sweet herbage and pure water of her mountain counties. In Monroe county, Ohio, only separated from West Virginia by the width of the river, a Swiss colony is engaged in the successful manufacture of an article of cheese imitation "Gruyere," commanding at wholesale from 18 to 20 cents per pound in the St. Louis or Cincinnati markets, where the demand far exceeds the supply.

HONEY.

Although bee culture flourishes here with but little care and labor, it is not yet carried on as an industrial pursuit. The total production in 1860 was only 423,-559 pounds, about 67,000 of which are credited to the county of Boone; the next largest producer, Wyoming county claiming only 19,067 pounds. If every farmers family in the State would keep half-a-dozen hives, yielding 200 pounds, the total production would reach ten million pounds. But in fact a much larger amount could be produced from the varied and beautiful flora of the forest and field, whose reign of bloom and fragrance extends from March to November, not to mention the blossoms of the orchard and garden.

On a majority of farms where bees are kept, the arrangements for that purpose are of the most primitive character, the old style gum or box hive, with a moveable cap, being the nearest approach to a "palace" yet accomplished. These rude habitations are generally placed on flat stones, or low wooden benches, and appear to answer the purpose as well as more intricate and costly innovations. In the season of the moth, the hives are raised an inch or two, so as to admit the brush underneath, and in the winter some additional shelter of plank is provided for protection from the severest weather. Beyond this, and housing young swarms, very little attention is paid to bee culture in West Virginia.

In the remotest sections, the present stock of bees was mainly propagated from wild swarms captured in the woods, where colonies also return when not cared for at the time of their exit from the mother hive. The native bee is remarkable for its industrious and peacable habits, and seldom uses its dart either for attack or defence.

The price of honey in the comb varies from 20 to 25 cents per pound, and the supply is very scarce throughout State.

MISCELLANEOUS CROPS.

Among the other productions of the field, returned by the census of 1860 we find:

RICE—1163 pounds, raised in the counties of Boone, Wood and Wetzel, as an experiment with no encouraging results. Natural swamps are too rare, and artificial irrigation too impracticable on undulating ground, for the successful cultivation of this crop.

COTTON is grown in an experimental way in a few counties South of the Great Kanawha, with moderate success, but will never become a staple production in this State.

HEMP succeeds as well here as in Kentucky or Missouri; but edible crops are more indispensible, and more remunerative in West Virginia.

FLAX succeeds very well in high or lowland in every part of the State. The production of 1860 is given at 183,498 pounds, but was probably increased threefold during the dearth of cotton, consequent upon the war. Flax is exclusively used in domestic manufactures and not known as an article of trade.

HOPS are as yet cultivated only for domestic purposes, the crop of 1860 not much exceeding 3000 pounds. This plant thrives luxuriantly wherever its seeds fall upon loose soil, but is not likely to become an object of more general cultivation, until the improved area of the State is greatly increased.

BROOM CORN is a sure crop wherever corn and sorghum are grown, but up to date only raised for home consumption.

MARKET GARDENING.

In a State destitute of populous cities, this department of rural industry is not expected to be extensively encouraged, yet even the present supply is far from meeting the demand for a variety of cheap vegetables and fruits, at the proper seasons. In the markets of Wheeling and Parkersburg prices are frequently as high if not higher, than in New York and Philadelphia, and the supply irregular and uncertain. An increased production and a reduction of from 25 to 50 per cent. would largely increase the consumption, and yet leave a fair profit for the producer.

The last Census gives the amount realized from market gardening at $44,299, which was evidently below the true figures at the time, and does not come up to one half of the present production. This branch is almost exclusively in the hands of small farmers near towns, who never made gardening a study, and for success, depend more upon favorable soil and climate, than upon science or skill. Hot houses for the production of vegetables out of season are very few in number, and quite indifferently managed.

The following are, in alphabetical order, the garden vegetables which attain perfection in the open air in every section of the State: Artichoke, Asparagus. Beans, Beet, Borecole, Broccoli, Brussels Sprouts, Cabbage, Carrots, Cauliflower, Celery, Cress, Cucumber, Eggplant, Endive, Gourd, Horse Radish, Jerusalem Artichoke, Lettuce, Love Apple, or Tomato, Mangel Wurzel, Melons of every known variety, Mustard, Okra, Oyster Plant, Onion, Parsley, Parsnip, Peas, Pepper, (red), Potato, Sweet Potato, Pumpkin, Radish, Rhubarb, Spinage, Squash, and every variety of the Turnip.

Culinary and medicinal household herbs: Aniseed, Caraway, Chamomile, Chervil, Chive, Coriander, Dandelion, Dill, Estragon, Garlic, Hyssop, Lavender, Leek, Marjoram, Mint, Rosemary, Rue, Sage, Paragon, Thyme and a number of others of minor utility.

What is said above in regard to price and supply of vegetables, is equally applicable to small or garden fruit. With the exception of currants, which thrive without scarcely any attention, all small fruits are higher than they should be, especially the strawberry and rhaspberry. Gooseberries are more abundant. Of blackberries, a few of the improved varieties have lately been introduced, but cannot compete in regard to price with the wild or native article, which luxuriates in every neglected field and fence corner, and yields but little to the improved sorts in size and quality. The other wild fruits found in the market at the proper season, are the huckle and whortleberry, dewberry, wild rhaspberry and wild cherry.

The cranberry is found growing wild on a few patches of undrained bogs in the mountain counties, but not of very good quality. Artificially it is not cultivated at all.

There is no doubt but that small fruit may be cultivated with profit for the Baltimore and Cincinnati markets all along the Baltimore & Ohio Railroad, and Ohio river, express transportation from that stream to Baltimore requiring but eighteen, and from the western base of the Alleghanies to Cincinnati not exceeding sixteen hours. When it will be generally known that improved lands, fertilized by the hand of nature, can be purchased here for this purpose at from $15 to 25, convenient to water and timber, there may be less demand for the sandy barrens of South Jersey, where *unimproved* lands requiring constant and expensive manuring are now being sold to fruit growers at the rate of $25 per acre.

In regard to poultry and eggs, the market is even more irregularly supplied than with any other commodity. Fat turkeys are seldom to be had at less than 18 cents per pound; chickens bring from 12½ to 15 per pound and eggs, from 15 to 20 cents per dozen in the summer, and from 25 to 35 cents in the winter.

Statement of the principal items of farm produce according to the Census of 1860.—Table A.

COUNTIES.	Wheat.	Indian Corn.	Oats.	Tobacco.	Irish Potatoes.	Slaughtered animals.
	Bushels.	*Bushels.*	*Bushels.*	*Pounds.*	*Bushels.*	*Value.*
Barbour	37,835	197,460	29,680	596	17,256	$53,452
Berkeley	237,576	275'525	76,176	....	13,962	93,555
Braxton	22,366	122,749	17,595	15,634	8,300	20,327
Brooke	23,490	142,122	94,984	....	20,488	36,763
{ Boone	15,278	143,808	7,994	18,729	10,620	30,879
{ Cabell	65,715	248,210	18,717	68,578	11,119	49,736
{ Lincoln (new)	....	....	....	....	....	....
Calhoun	10,734	69,847	6,423	7,882	6,088	13.455
Clay	4,433	44,310	6,150	26,229	4.269	12,597
Doddridge	16,514	124,133	6,765	7,025	13,724	24.848
Fayette	25,693	131,425	28,433	127,713	10,223	44,107
Gilmer	18,609	126,944	11,800	61,104	7,836	21,167
Greenbrier	52,017	231,479	112,055	3,000	24,858	114,265
{ Hampshire	106,310	375,090	49,259	.75	41,773	109,834
{ Mineral (new)	....	....	....	....	....	....
Hancock	16,423	61,316	46,716	....	26,002	26,396
{ Hardy	39,046	286,618	20,200	1,450	18,534	71,698
{ Grant (new)	....	....	....	....	....	....
Harrison	55,411	320,946	37,501	11,715	15,357	75,883
Jackson	88,338	219,377	11,878	74,691	32,630	40,260
Jefferson	422,514	358,267	54,798	6,700	31,876	110,221
Kanawha	76,305	274'943	45,430	338,264	12,352	56,345
Lewis	27,191	136,677	12,418	82,910	9,822	.28,817
Logan	11,025	199,385	11,067	13,545	9,794	30,559
Marion	50,894	214,706	85,409	25,012	12,618	55,990
Marshall	74,759	241,911	133,617	10,590	46,634	44,944
Mason	108,839	264,813	6,462	21,996	11,873	55,706
Mercer	43,131	131,654	55,843	182,554	10,533	58,132
Monongalia	49,134	239,024	126,198	1,380	10,586	46,994
Monroe	84,805	216.513	59,265	132;019	12,692	78,506
Morgan	19,404	47,575	10,122	2,234	7,806	21,323
McDowell	1,041	20,445	2,215	1,275	1,410	8,138
Nicholas	12,894	103,193	26,613	14,470	15,528	64,227
Ohio	20,048	138,430	82,101	....	21,449	26,930
Pendleton	11,475	122,997	16,516	2,073	13,366	45,319
Pocahontas	8,774	48,229	26,412	190	12,090	41,554
Preston	8,933	71,063	104,317	185	44,655	80,407
Putnam	78,796	197,700	16,355	406,992	9,192	57,165
Pleasants	22,785	102,172	7,395	27,930	7,747	15,284
Raleigh	6,700	39,301	11,713	34,827	3,719	13,363
Randolph	7,675	56,225	20,248	1,117	8,349	24,883
Ritchie	27,582	147,785	14,978	18,606	19,490	35.763
Roane	21,897	100,074	8,743	10,268	6,593	20,571
Taylor	20,811	78,001	25,610	3,139	4,294	22,383
Tucker	1,103	19,955	6,049	710	4,346	7,721
Tyler	43,727	182,239	28,512	11,225	23,733	25,150
Upshur	27,765	149,496	20,337	50,000	13,639	35,217
Wayne	35,319	224,044	13,077	55,628	8,898	40,141
Webster	1,586	25,602	3,100	....	2,194	6,439
Wetzel	31,652	180,150	26,775	84,989	14,430	28,182
Wirt	27.488	115,046	5,096	44,074	8,769	22,749
Wood	74,236	227,223	19,158	166,365	33,166	51,682
Wyoming	5,601	62,420	9,515	4,778	4,024	19,740
	2,302,567	7,858,647	1,649,090	2,180,316	746,606	$0,124,829

STOCK FARMING.

The practical farmer who has attentively perused the preceding chapters has already arrived at the conclusion that if any one section of the United States is better suited than another in regard to climate, soil and location to the successful growing of live stock, that section must embrace West Virginia, and portions of adjoining States similarly situated. Until recently, when the mineral excitement built up mushroom fortunes among us, the great bulk of the private wealth in this State was the more or less direct product of this branch of rural economy, which supports and vitalizes every other. Stockfarming, in short, is the pulsating artery of agricultural prosperity in West Virginia, and it is by her natural capacity in this line, and by no other standard, that her future *agricultural* development may be estimated with any degree of accuracy,

If the surface of the State were smoother for the plough, her lands would be equal in price to those of Maryland and Pennsylvania. On the other hand they would be equally exposed to be impoverished by overcropping, and perhaps exhausted and untenanted like those of our mother State, Virginia, while as a stock region she may preserve her virginal freshness for ages. It may be safely asserted, that her surface, rough as it comparatively is, will in the long run, produce larger returns than the smoother lands of the adjoining States, in proportion to capital and labor invested, *provided it be devoted to the purpose for which it is manifestly intended by nature.*

In the production of live stock, West Virginia figures in the Census of 1860, with $12,382,680, ranking above New Hampshire, Minnesota, Kansas, Oregon, California, Connecticut, Delaware, Rhode Island, and coming within $250,000 of the production of Massachusetts. This was ten years ago. Since then at the usual rate of progression, those figures should have increased by one-fourth, but, allowing for the prostration of agriculture during the late war, and the large export of every description of stock to the depleted South, since its close, it is doubtful whether the next Census will confirm this estimate, unless it be through the unprecedented increase of prices during the last five years. At any rate the stock business has never been more flourishing than at present, judging from the anxiety of our graziers to increase their landed estates. There is apparently more money made and circulated in this than any other branch of husbandry, and no matter how hard the times, or how dull other trades, whenever ready cash is wanted, live stock, in any stage of growth, is sure to command it.

One-half of the live stock in the State in 1860, or about $6,000,000, was owned in the counties of Barbour, Harrison, Hampshire, Greenbrier, Monroe, Hardy, Jefferson, Marion, Monongalia and Preston. In these counties, to which may be added Brooke, Doddridge, Hancock, Jackson, Lewis, Marshall, Mason, Mercer, Pocahontas, Pendleton, Ohio, Nicholas, Randolph, Taylor and Upshur are to be found the most extensive and productive grazing farms, as well the best breeds of live stock of every description. Considering that in a more advanced state of improvement in land and stock, the amount of live stock may be doubled in each of the ten first named counties, and there is not a single county too small or too poor to yield the same results, the figure of $50,000,000 as the the total value of live stock in the State is only a question of time.

HORSES AND MULES.

Assessing the 85,862 horses, young and old, footed up in Table B. at an average price of $65 per head, we obtain $5,581,030, or nearly one-half of the total value of the live stock in the State. This is a large proportion, considering that breeding for sale is not carried on as a business. Every farmer seeks to raise his own work stock, and from time to time disposes of his surplus increase. Horses are not regarded as profitable to grow, unless of superior blood, or if sold young, before the animal "eats its head off," as it is termed, on the farm. One hundred dollars is, at present, a fair price for an ordinary farm horse in the prime of life. From that up to $200 is paid for improved grades, or greater speed and symmetry of form, for export to Eastern markets, among others the tide water region of Virginia. The breed of horses throughout the State was notably improved within the last twenty years by importations from Ohio and Kentucky. Northern breeds have not yet been introduced to any extent, though grades of Morgan and Canadian are now more frequently met with than formerly.

Horses reared in West Virginia with any degree of care, are remarkable for bottom, wind, spirited action, surefootedness and docility. If well attended the first winter, they require very little or no grain feeding until old enough for use, and sustain themselves one-half of that time, in good order, on short commons or woods pasture.

Asses are as yet sparsedly represented, the total number of asses and mules being reported at $18,000. Much the greater portion of the mules in the State were imported from Kentucky and Tennessee. Although a mule is reared here almost as cheaply as a steer, yet owing to an inveterate prejudice of our yeomanry against the paternal parent, breeding this class of stock is not very popular. A serviceable mule brings here from $150 to $200. A large number of those on hand now were, left here by the army at the close of the war.

Turf Associations, or Jockey Clubs have been in operation for some years at Wheeling and Parkeısburg, but, as their object is not the improvement of the horse for practical purposes, their utility is very questionable.

MILCH COWS.

Milch cows form an important item in the list of live stock, their aggregate in the State being put down at 100,154 head, or three cows for every two families in town and county. The average value probably not exceeds $35 per head, although in the more level and best improved counties there are animals of superior grades at from $50 to $75 per head. But few probably exceed the latter figure. In the interior and more hilly sections, the native breed is still preferred, as best adapted to the circumstances of the country. This breed generally termed "our common stock," runs through all the varieties of the long-horned and loose jointed type, whose pedigree is accident and confusion; yet, as it furnishes by far better milkers than Devon, Durham, or graded cows on the same keep, it is not likely to be discarded soon. The Ayrshires, Holstein and Jersey breeds would probably prove equal, if not superior to the native stock, as milkers, but possess no advantage over it as breeders for beef cattle, which is a paramount consideration here. The common cow is generally gentle, easily kept, perfectly at home in the hills and woods, where, if necessary, she will support herself during six months of the year, while suckling a calf, with milk to spare, and come to her winter quarters in prime condition. During the winter season she needs no stabling, at least she seldom gets any, an open shed answering all purposes in stormy weather.

As a rule, cows are not kept for breeding purposes exclusively, and even in West Virginia, this would be unprofitable on a large scale, except in connection with a dairy, the returns of which would repay at least the keeping of the cow, leaving the calf as net profit. As a consequence, the supply of native stock is not sufficient for the wants of the graziers, who make up the deficiency by purchases in adjoining States, principally Ohio. Stockcattle of all grades and ages are bought up, and grazed in West Virginia uutil ready for market. Some dealers, who cut large crops of hay, winter extensive herds of mixed ages; others confine themselves more particularly to grazing three year old steers up to market order, and winter but little, beginning to ship in June and ending in November. Grainfeeding, for later use, is principally confined to the Ohio river and Potomac counties. In sections where pasture, especially blue grass, has been economized in the fall, fattening steers are turned on grass as early as March, and mature in June or July. This mode of operation, while requiring the least labor, unquestionably yields the largest profit, in proportion to the period of investment, frequently 50 per cent. on the cost of the animal in the spring; but to pursue it on a large scale, requires an abundance of first class sod, conveniently partitioned off to afford change of pasture.

Within the last fifteen or twenty years the native stock of cattle has been materially improved by crossing with Shorthorns, Devons and grades of these breeds. On lowland farms, with good winter accommodations, and an abundance of feed at all times, the Durham matures with profit to the owner; but the neat, compact and nimble Devon is the animal for our hills, which he climbs with the agility of a sheep, thriving as he goes. Crosses of Devon and common stock are fast being introduced in every section of the State, and West Virginia beef cattle are successfully competing with the product of other States in the Baltimore market, where, requiring but a few hours transportation, they reach in superior condition.

Mr. Dodge refers to a circular sent ont in 1854 by the Agricultural Division of the Patent Office, inquiring the cost of raising stock in different sections of the country. The cost of a steer three years old was reported to be $25 in New York, $24 in Ohio, $15 in Illinois, $12 in Iowa, and but $8 in West Virginia. The latter figure, even at that time, and under the most favorable circumstances was certainly a very low estimate. Allowing nothing for the keep of the cow during the *dry* period of gestation, and putting the calf's keep of the first year at $6, of the second at $8 and of the third at $10, we reach $24. This figure, which includes the producers cost and profit, is as little as would *now* be taken by the producer for the lightest three year old, not absolutely dwarfed. Good yearlings—really from 18 to 22 months old—in common wintering order, are bringing now (Nov. 1869) from $17 to $22, and two year olds—from 30 to 32 months—from $35 to 45 per head. The profit of him who grazes for market, depends upon the weight he may put upon the animal between spring and fall. Estimates based upon hypothetical premises, are omitted here, as they do not satisfy the practical operator, who knows how much depends upon economical management, and good judgment in buying and selling—an art by the way—in which West Virginia traders have nothing to learn from the rest of mankind.

The cost of grazing stock is materially reduced, when cattle are summered in the woods during the second and third year, with no other trouble and expense than occasional looking up and salting. Where pea vine, and other succulent herbage abounds, as in the greater portion of the State, the results in growth and flesh compare favorably with those of field pasturing, though less tallow may be formed. In the Kanawha Valley and the counties South of it, winter feeding is considerably shortened by the mildness of the season and, sometimes entirely dispensed with. The writer remembers meeting a herd of two year old steers, browsing in the wilds of Logan county, about the middle of January, looking but little the worse in flesh, though horns and limbs seemed to have gained somewhat the advantage over the carcass in the race for existence.

In the chapter of climate, reference was made to the duration of winterfeeding in the mountain counties. In the remainder of the State it varies from three to five months, the longest period being required in all cases where no pasture is at hand in open weather. The feeding is generally done in the open field, either from the stack in the meadows, or in out fields, where the shattering grass seed, or the manure of the stock may be wanted. Stock cattle seldom have any sheds to run to, but are accustomed to "rough it" under the lee of hills, or timber, as best they may.

Many farmers in the older counties are in the habit of sending their stock to be summered in the woods, in distant and less improved sections, under the care of some settler of the locality. Others use for that purpose the, so-called "mountain farms" on the table lands of Randolph, Pocahontas, Webster, Nicholas, Greenbrier, &c., under the supervision of the work hands engaged in fencing and clearing up the ground. These mountain farms, which produce the finest beef and mutton in the State, are generally improved at a comparatively trifling cost. The price of the lands seldom exceeds $1.50 per acre. After constructing a worm fence at a cost of $2 per acre, or less, according to the area enclosed, the largest timber is girdled, or "deadened," at an expense of from 50 cents to $1 per acre, making the cost of the improvement, say $4.50 per acre, land included. The girdled timber dies during the first year, letting in the light and heat necessary to vegetation. Where neither oak or hickory grow, no undergrowth is to be found either before or after the clearing, and the first thing that comes up after the deadening, is a thick growth of blackberry briers, which will completely die out within two years, or sooner, if cattle are turned in to keep them down. By that time the native, spontaneous blue grass has taken complete possession of the surface, and the farm is ready to yield a perennial pasture, worth for each season, at least $4 per acre. In the course of a few years, the girdled timber has dried sufficiently to burn in the log, so soon as cut down, requiring no piling up in heaps. The cost of the final operation varies with the size and amount of timber, from $2 to $2.50 per acre.

In the remainder of the State, where undergrowth prevails more or less, repeated grubbing is necessary to make a clean field, but when the land is required for rough grazing alone, and not for the plough, a less expensive process is frequently resorted to, called "hacking," which consists in chopping off brushwood and saplings from two to three feet above the ground. When this operation is performed during the first three days after full moon in June, July or August—especially June—it is said to be more effectual than at any other time, and without pretending to account for the fact, the writer is enabled to confirm it by his own experience. A majority of the brush generally dies off within the first year, and the after-sprouts of the remainder are easily destroyed by cattle and sheep, in course of a short time.

Another popular mode of preparing land for pasture consists in grubbing out thoroughly everything under the "size of a man's arm," and then feeding out hay upon the ground during the winter to scatter the seed. In early spring all the timber not wanted for fencing and other purposes, is cut down for browse, and permitted to lie as it falls for a few years, until the limbs are rotten or tramped down by the grazing stock, when fire is set to the trunks in seasons of leisure, and the last snag is reduced to ashes. Land, prepared in this way, is considerably enriched by the decaying limbs and bark, and the ashes of the trunks, and produces the freshest and most durable pasture.

In this rough manner the oldest and most extensive grazing farms were originally cleared, and gradually enriched their owners. Fortunes of from $50,000 to $150,000 were accumulated in the live stock business by men, who started in life as common farm hands, and began their independent career with a brace of calves.

SHEEP HUSBANDRY.

It was settled some years ago, after protracted and learned exchange of opinions, that sheep raising or woolgrowing is profitable in the Northern States, notwithstanding the high price of land, and the rigors of climate. And an eminent authority in the matter, Dr. Henry S. Randall, has proved in a series of letters, exhaustive upon the subject, that it is equally profitable in the South, despite the high temperature, and deficiency in herbage. The writer might therefore be dispensed with the task of demonstrating the success of this pastoral pursuit in an intermediate section, not liable to the objections raised against either extremes, and surpassing both in natural advantages most essential to success.

Nor does the writer's official correspondence with strangers, seeking information upon the resources of this State, indicate that there is any doubt upon this point in any part of the world. On the contrary, it appears to be a proposition universally conceded, that if sheep-husbandry is not profitable in West Virginia, it were useless to attempt it in any other locality; and inquiry seems to turn mainly upon the questions: What breeds of sheep are best suited to the country? Which is the most appropriate mode of management? And why the business is not carried on to a much greater extent?

Sheep husbandry was among the first necessities of the early settlers, who were confined to this resource for the greater part of their wearing and household apparel. No other branch of rural economy was so well suited their comfortable habits, as the care of sheep, which scarcely required any care at all, at least so far as food and shelter were concerned. But there were other drawbacks which prevented their flocks from assuming patriarchal dimensions; and those were the migratory habits of the animal—scattering and straying—the depredations of wolves, and lastly, sheep killing dogs.

In the course of the improvement of the country, these obstacles were gradually overcome with nearly complete success. The county premiums on scalps have driven the wolves to their last ditch. A wise law passed in 1863 puts the dogs upon their good behavior, and neighbors have settled down sufficiently close, to keep an obliging eye on each others flocks.

From the nature of the difficulties referred to, the older and most improved sections took the lead in the rearing of sheep, and of 453,334 head reported in the State in 1860, one-fourth were owned in the Panhandle counties, Brooke, Ohio, Hancock and Marshall. The counties next in in rank are Hampshire and Preston, with about 20,000 head each, then Greenbrier with 16,000, and Pendleton with 14,000, then follows Harrison, Pocahontas, Monroe, Mercer, Monongalia, Barbour and Hardy with from 10,000 to 12,000 each. The remaining counties numbered respectively, from 9000 to 853, the latter figure being the quota of the new county of McDowell, on the Southern border of the State. The Auditor's Report for 1868, returns 568,563 head of sheep, an increase of 115,229, or one-fourth, since 1860.

The aggregate clip of wool for the year 1860, is given at 1,063,163 pounds, or an average of 2 pounds 6 ounces per head, including lambs not sheared. Deducting one-third for lambs, or 151,111 head, leaves 302,223 head of sheared sheep, and brings up the average weight of fleece to a fraction over 3½ pounds, which, considering that the average of Ohio is 4.05 and of Pennsylvania 5.36 (fractions in decimals) would appear a somewhat low estimate without some explanation. In the four Panhandle counties above named, the total number of sheep is 112,094; making the usual deduction of one-third for lambs not sheared, gives 74,730 sheared sheep and increases the average weight of fleece to 4.04 pounds, equal to the average in the State of Ohio. Yet even this figure cannot be taken as a criterion of the capacity of West Virginia, for, although the the Panhandle boasts of the most improved breeds, the cleanest sheep walks, and the most intelligent and enterprising sheep growers in the State, flocks and fixtures have not yet reached the degree of perfection to which the public spirited people of that section are unceasingly aspiring, and what can be done there, may be done elsewhere in the State as well.

The favorite breeds in that section, at present, are the Merinos, Saxon, and their grades, improved by frequent importations from New York, Vermont and New Hampshire. Wool is the object here, mutton merely incidental. It is the product of this section which has principally given character and reputation to West Virginia wool. Within a few years past, long wooled sheep have also been introduced with complete success, and among others, one sale is reported of Cotswold staple averaging 9 pounds per fleece, on a good sized flock.

Mr. Dodge calls attention to the fact that sheep husbandry has proved a source of large profit in those four counties, on land valued at from $20 to $44 per acre, but really worth from $50 to $100 per acre, and that the other products of the soil, far from suffering from the preponderance of sheep, are thereby increased; concluding, very pertinently, that the flocks of the farm add more to its fertility than they subtract from it.

In a number of the next largest wool growing counties, Harrison, Taylor, Barbour and Lewis among the rest, Southdowns, Cotswolds, and their grades, are found in considerable numbers along with some very superior flocks of Merino and other fine wool grades. The larger and longer wooled sheep are regarded as preferable for wool and mutton combined, and their fleece is better adapted to the machinery in use here than the finer grades. Cotswold fleeces are reported from Harrison of from 5 to 7 pounds, and Cotswold mutton sheep were shipped from the same locality, worth at the scales at Clarksburg, $14 per head.

The price of Panhandle wool has varied within the last ten years from 50 to 75 cents per pound, and the product of the next best wool growing counties, from 35 to 60 cents. The wool of the common native stock, of which there are many grades with occasionally a sprinkling of Merino, has varied from 25 to 40 cents, unwashed. It is a matter of general surprise, that the quality of the common wool has not more seriously deteriorated under the careless, not to say barbarous treatment of sheep, in the newer and more remote sections. There, after shearing about the middle of May, young and old are turned upon the commons, or into the woods, and scarcely ever seen again until fall, except when coming home or hunted up to be salted. About the first snow, if it happens to set in with a severe storm, they are let in upon a short grazed, half cleared woods pasture, where they spend the winter, receiving only a scant allowance of corn fodder, with an occasional nubbin for the bearing ewes toward lambing time. For the latter an open shed is sometimes provided, and the owner thinks he is doing uncommonly well, when the ewes survive the maternal crisis without a loss of more than one lamb out of three. In the absence of any system, lambing time comes in at any season, usually, as luck would have it, in the roughest "spell" in January, and continues until Spring, the latest lambs generally catching up in growth with the stunted firstlings in a few weeks.

Out of a hundred such cases which came under the observation of the writer, one experience may be selected from one of the central counties, and given in the party's own words: "I generally graze from 300 to 400 head of cattle, and winter from 200 to 300. I have no particular fancy for sheep, but I keep about 300 head, common stock, with a few grade bucks among them. They range, the whole year round, in fenced woodland, with here and there a half cleared patch to run to, where I sometimes leave some salt for them, and they can lick the ashes of the burned timber, when I don't. In the winter they shift for themselves, trimming off the sprouts in clearings and fence corners, until the snow is too deep to paw through, when I let them into the meadow where the cattle are fed. Some eat the hay, and some don't; sheep are not very fond of it. I have no leisure to look after them in lambing time, and they must do the best they can. Some of the lambs come dead born, others freeze to death, and the foxes get their share. *I take what's left.* When I gather up the flock in shearing time, I generally find from 75 to 100 lambs able to get along. My clip is about 7 or 800 pounds of wool, worth from 30 to 35 cents per pound. In August I sell off about 75 or 100 mutton sheep at an average of $2.50 pêr head, which, together with the wool, is clear profit, as the flock pays for its support in keeping down the brush and manuring and *sodding* the land."

Here is a net profit of $450 or $1.50 per head, say one hundred per cent. per annum on the capital invested. This man, who began the world with an axe and a few calves, has accumulated at least $75,000 by grazing alone; as a "cattle man" and a shrewd dealer he probably has no superior in the State. He took the premium at the last Harrison County Agricultural Fair, for the best steer, but has evidently "no fancy for sheep."

But it is not necessary to demonstrate the profits of sheep husbandry in West Virginia, by instances of such *rigorous* economy. Here is an example a of little milder sort, from the adjoining county of Ritchie:

"I keep about 500 head of sheep, and from 30 to 50 head of cattle. The sheep are mostly a cross of common stock with grade Merino; good sized animals, profitable for both mutton and wool. So long as they can stand it out doors, I herd them about in the open woods; am never more than two or three days out of sight of them, and salt them regularly. Never had any loss from straying or disease, and but little from dogs. Early in the winter, I turn them into my pastures and meadows, giving the best fields to ewes in lamb. I never feed much of either hay or fodder, unless the snow is too deep to paw through, which doesn't occur very often. Towards lambing time, the ewes have the sheds and barns to run to, and get a handfull of shell corn, or twice that amount of oats a piece, per day. I save most all my lambs, except in case of triplets or unavoidable accidents, and get about 125 from every 100 ewes. The wethers and dry ewes are turned upon the commons again early in April, and the ewes with lambs kept in until shearing time. I generally get from 3 to 5 pounds of wool per head, the largest fleeces from two year old wethers; all of it worth from 30 to 40 cents per pound, unwashed, burs and all. I sell off the fat wethers and dry ewes every fall, say about 300 head, at an average of $2.25 per head."

This man values his time in tending the flock at $100, the winter feed and pasture at $200, which counting $700 for $2000 pounds of wool at 35 cents, and $675 for 300 mutton sheep at 2.25, leaves a margin of $1,075 on 500 sheep, or 65 cents more per head than in the preceeding case, besides the improvement of his fields from manures, which this party says, he could not realize so cheaply from any other source.

These results are obtained on lands worth in a state of nature from $2 to $3 per acre in more remote sections, and should induce woolgrowers who meet in Convention to memorialize Congress for an increase of the tariff, to sell out their $50 to $100 per acre estates, and remove to the spot where their industry flourishes without so much protection.

Since the above was written the following appeared in the *Ravenswood* (Jackson Co.) *News:*

Fine Region for Wool Growing.—It is the opinion of men experienced in woolgrowing, that the hills and valleys of Jackson County are well adapted to that business. Mr. John P. Campbell, formerly of Hancock County in this State, is so well convinced that it will be profitable here, that, last summer he brought from that country nearly 200 fine sheep which have fed and prospered, on a tract of land lying near the head springs of the Turkey Fork of Sandy Creek, in Jackson and Raone counties, bought by him last spring. They have lived entirely, on wild pea vines and grass growing in the timber, and are in excellent condition. Last week, we saw in the stable of the St. Charles Hotel here, three Merino bucks, recently bought by him in Hancock, at a price, which if disclosed, would astonish some of the farmers of Jackson county. In Hancock and Brooke, wool growers frequently pay from fifty to one hundred dollars each, for bucks, which are considered cheap at that. Mr. Campbell believes that since wool growing is profitable in those counties on farms which are worth $75 per acre, it must pay where land naturally as good, can be had for less than one-fourth that sum. We think his logic is sound; and it is corroborated by the fact, that our winters are several weeks shorter than theirs.

HOG RAISING.

In the early stage of the settlement of the country, hog raising is said to have been much more extensively and profitably followed than at present, owing to the low price of corn, in the absence of a market, and to the almost unlimited ranges of woodland, abounding, at least biennially, in masts of acorn, hickory, chesnut and beech. Even as late as 25 years ago, corn did not bring over 25 cents per bushel in West Virginia; and 2½ to 3 cents gross for pork, was then regarded as a remunerative price. Now corn averages 80 cents throughout the year, and fat hogs do not bring over 7 to 7½ cents gross, leaving the chances of the market in favor of corn in the grain.

This change in value appears to have exerted its influence upon the production of hogs, in which a notable decrease is perceptible, even without the aid of accurate statistical information. The total number of swine is reported by the Census of 1860 as 427,214 or 1 1-7 to each inhabitant. This is a large figure, implying a surplus for exportation. With few exceptions, the crop of hogs, taken by counties, was then nearly in proportion to population and the production of corn. The State Auditor reports only 180,732 head for 1868, and shows considerable shifting of the sources of production. Thus in 1860 the counties of Berkely, Greenbrier, Hampshire, Harrison, Jefferson, Kanawha, Mercer, Monroe and Nicholas return from 10,000 to 15,000 each, Jefferson taking the lead. According to the Auditor's Report Jefferson is still ahead with 10,649, but the next largest producers in 1866 are Boone 7,786, Cabell 5,598, Kanawha 4,394, Marshall 4,291, while Nicholas returns only 3174 against 12,390 in 1860, and the remaining counties occupy the scale from 3159 (Wirt) down to 246 (Brooke), the latter having figured up 3309 head in 1860. In the absence of sufficient reliability in the Assessor's returns, it is not safe to speculate upon the causes of these apparent differences, though the decrease, independently of under returns, may be accounted for by the improved price and home market for corn, while the shifting of the sources of production may have followed as a natural consequence, at least to some extent. One thing, however, is certain, that if raising hogs does not pay so well now as formerly, that which produces pork, namely, corn, amply makes up the difference in the sum of production, saving the trouble and risk of the fattening operation.

In mast years the production of the back connties is always notably increased. When, duriug the intervening periods the supply of stock hogs is larger than can be fattened on grain, the surplus is allowed to root for dear life, until acorns come again.

In default of accurate statistics, it is not possible to know the relation between the exportation of pork and the importation of bacon. Large droves are continually shipped to the East for the want of adequate packing facilities in the State, and on the other hand no inconsiderable amount of bacon, mainly Cincinnati cured, is brought into our towns, and manufacturing and mining centers. Bacon of country production being rather indifferently put up, in comparison with city cured, does not command the same price by 5 or 10 per cent. The pork packing business is, so far, confined to the cities of Wheeling, Parkersburg and Point Pleasant, and its annual extent is materially controlled by the prospects of the market at the time.

Number and value of live stock—Census of 1860.—Table B.

COUNTIES.	Horses.	Milch Cows.	W'k oxen and other Cattle.	Sheep.	Swine.	Value of live stock.
Barbour	3,059	3,726	8,133	11,673	9;916	$377,693
Berkeley	3,510	2,728	3,699	7,057	13,469	335,757
Boone	787	I,444	3,506	3,248	7,653	120,589
Braxton	976	1,395	1,923	6,108	5,040	109,456
Brooke	1,399	1,319	1,682	40,620	3,309	282,439
Cabell	1,350	1,475	4,636	5,764	8,408	195,674
Calhoun	484	741	1,735	2,412	2,956	74,651
Clay	289	538	787	1,608	2,412	41,824
Doddridge	1,182	1,664	3,379	5,377	4,332	142,269
Fayette	1,266	1,767	2,938	6,998	7,723	177,440
Gilmer	815	1,197	2,597	3,967	3,864	113,722
Greenbrier	3,714	3,984	8,759	16,067	10,971	676,298
Hampshire	5,222	5,522	11,361	21,287	14,619	763,454
Hancock	1,109	1,127	1,797	21,402	2,465	182,746
Hardy	2,526	2,561	8,386	11,378	7,032	453,768
Harrison	5,404	4,501	18,244	13,202	11,496	644,325
Jackson	1,330	1,541	3,017	6,615	6,538	173,354
Jefferson	3,421	2,316	4,206	7,269	15,044	466,168
Kanawha	1,402	1,889	4,329	4,936	10,135	197,224
Lewis	1,617	1,902	4,340	8,250	4,554	225,500
Logan	885	1,595	4,340	4,673	9,197	161,480
Marion	3,762	4,629	6,334	9,029	9,985	466,254
Marshall	2,413	2,501	3,686	10,022	8,447	280,860
Mason	1,355	1,254	3,882	5,582	8,294	252,063
Mercer	I,552	2,218	4,327	10,225	11,308	244,954
Monongalia	3,904	3,881	7,770	10,845	8,028	454,070
Monroe	3,216	3,058	9,588	12,288	10.172	500,268
Morgan	972	1,036	1.725	2,992	3,300	111,439
McDowell	222	573	810	866	2,463	33,785
Nicholas	1,358	1,728	5,028	9,093	12,390	334,820
Ohio	1,441	1,408	1,626	40,050	3,244	253,090
Pendleton	2,543	3,423	6,383	14,143	5,744	371,228
Pocahontas	1,688	2,447	5,717	10,338	5,099	321,002
Preston	3,326	4,993	6,437	19,084	8,854	461,133
Putnam	1,229	1,509	3,815	5,924	8,084	188,995
Pleasants	646	725	1,511	2,837	2,386	84,275
Raleigh	486	744	1,439	3,569	3,663	69,038
Randolph	1,189	1,760	6,343	7,565	3,267	244,857
Ritchie	1,724	2,117	3,801	7,925	7,891	213,147
Roane	783	1,011	1,872	5,190	4,380	86,180
Taylor	1,137	1,347	2,940	4,788	3,710	162,804
Tucker	448	536	1,415	2,651	1,291	58,850
Tyler	1,484	1,644	3,305	8,748	5,942	202,707
Upshur	1,955	2,508	4,995	9,821	5,078	271,523
Wayne	1,240	1,524	1,939	7,405	8,898	175,008
Webster	356	693	1,061	2,474	1,691	44,304
Wetzel	1,502	1,806	3,421	6.244	6,293	169,639
Wirt	874	1,086	1,899	5,032	4,188	110,417
Wood	1,899	2,197	3,344	7,360	7,258	214,077
Wyoming	414	868	2,464	1,233	4,733	81,992
	85,862	100,154	209,935	453,334	427,214	12,382,680

New counties, from Auditors Report 1868. GRANT formed in 1868, from Hardy, 3816 head of milch cows, oxen and other cattle, 8167 sheep, 10,113 swine. LINCOLN formed in 1867 from Boone, Cabell, Logan and Kanawha, 2469 cattle, 3153 sheep, 1523 swine. MINERAL, formed in 1866 from Hampshire, 4154 cattle 5877 sheep, 654 swine.

FRUIT GROWING.

The reputation of West Virginia, as a fruit region, dates from the early stages of the settlement of the country. Seeds, carelessly dropped into the earth by the pioneers, rapidly grew up into luxuriant proportions, and brought forth varieties of fruit of which many, not inferior to improved sorts from other States, are propagated to this day by grafting. Improved varieties from the East and North were subsequently introduced, and are now flourishing more or less in every county. A number of sorts were even improved in size and flavor, and none are known to have failed in consequence of migration. Such is the geniality of the climate and the diversity of soil and exposure, that any kind of fruit of the temperate zone is naturalized here without difficulty.

The earliest efforts in fruit growing in the State were confined to apples and peaches, the latter producing so abundantly, that untold quantities were annually wasted for the want of labor to take care of crops; and even hogs, turned promiscuously into the orchards and lanes, were inadequate to the task of cleaning up the falling fruit. Since the last twenty years, however, the peach crop, as elsewhere in the United States, has become more uncertain, and a full crop does not occur more than once in two or three years, except under more careful cultivation than was formerly in use, and in favorable elevated exposures where the bloom is retarded. The largest and most certain crops are now yielded South of a line running very nearly with the Little Kanawha, and including the counties of Wirt, Calhoun, Gilmer, Braxton and Webster, where drying and canning for sale is carried on quite extensively. In the older counties, North of that line, much attention has been given to improved varieties, and there are bounteous harvests of luscious fruit in favorable seasons. Apples are at home in every nook and corner of the State, without regard to altitude, though some levels and exposures are better adapted to certain varieties than others. In the Ohio and Kanawha valleys, and along the lines of transportation, apples have been for many years a considerable article of export, thousands of barrels being annually shipped to the Pittsburg, Cincinnati and even to New Orleans and intermediate markets, and no matter how abundant the supply in the fall, the time has never been when the demand could be met in the Spring. In the interior, where there is no market for green fruit, large quantities are dried and distilled, fed to hogs, and wagon loads given away to new settlers, and even to old ones too indolent to plant their own trees. Excellent cider is also manufactured in the principal valleys, and the crab cider from Blannerhassets Island, near Parkersburg, enjoys more than a local reputation.

The most popular and successful varieties of the apple introduced up to date, are the Fall and Winter Rambo, Golden, Mammoth, Green, White and Newtown Pippins, Rhode Island Greening, Baldwin, Yellow Bellflower, Roxbury and Putnam Russets, Van de Wert Sweet Russet, Romanite, Rome Beauty, Northern Spy, Seeknofurther, Summer and Winter Pearmain, Smith's Cider, Grindstone Pippin, Porter, Wine Sap, Yellow Harvest, June Eating, Summer Sweet, Red Harvest, and several varieties of native summer fruit, not identifiable by name.

Of Peaches the Georges the IV, Morris White, Heath's Cling, Grosse Mignonne, Early York, Large White Cling, Crawford's Late, Early Scarlet, and are generally favorites.

Pears are not yet cultivated to any extent, and appear to thrive best in old improved localities. Bartlett and Seekel give general satisfaction, either as dwarf or standard. Dwarf pears of other varieties are slowly gaining ground.

The other fruits more or less disseminated all over the State are the Quince, the Apricot and almost every variety of Cherries and Plums cultivated in the Middle States. The German Plum, or French Prune is just becoming popular and yields well.

A serious obstacle to the propagation of improved fruit in West Virginia is the want of nurseries in convenient localities. Some very reliable establishments on the Ohio side, below Parkersburg, and at Moundsville, West Virginia, have hitherto furnished a large amount of trees to the remotest sections of the State; but their production is entirely inadequate to the present demand, and our farmers were frequently induced to purchase from Northern agents, principally of the Rochester nurseries, whose trees arrive in very indifferent condition, and do not always turn out as labeled. Three or four nurseries, at least, established at accessible points in different parts of the State, and giving their attention not only to trees, but to small fruit and grape vines, could rely upon a thriving business within a few years.

The Census of 1860 gives the value of orchard products in the State at about $230,000, not including the populous counties of Berkeley, Greenbrier, Mercer and the *peach* county of Webster, which seem to have been omitted in the returns under this head. The largest returns are from the counties of Cabell, Hamshire, Marion, Marshall, Ohio, Tyler, respectively from $10,000 to $15,000. But the utter unreliability of these returns is shown by the fact, that 3 or 4 of the most highly improved counties figure in the table with less than $100 each. It seems, moreover, extremely difficult to arrive at anything like correct estimates in regard to a product, of which such a large proportion is consumed or wasted without count or measure.

GRAPE CULTURE.

The culture of the vine became an object of interest in Western Virginia, soon after its success was established in the vicinity of Cincinnati, and the first vineyard seems to have been planted by Mr. C. L. Zane, on Zane's Island, opposite the city of Wheeling. The results obtained by this pioneer, said to have averaged 500 gallons of wine per acre, encouraged the establishment of a number of vineyards in Ohio county, whose production in 1865 is reported 50,000 gallons, and in 1868 at 150,000 gallons.

In the chapter on climate, it is shown that the whole of West Virginia is situated within the thermal zone in which the grape matures, with enough sunny days to spare between late spring and early fall frosts, to secure superior strength and quality to the wine.

On a surface so diversified as that of our State, it would be difficult to survey off a one hundred acre tract anywhere, without including at least one suitable exposure for a vineyard of from five to twenty acres, either in the valleys, or on slopes of from five to twenty-five degrees. German wine growers, who prefer steeper grades, will find the rock necessary for walling up, a few feet below the surface everywhere.

While every character of West Virginia soil, whether limestone, clay loam, calcareous, sandy and gravelly loam, vegetable mould or alluvial, appear to be almost equally well adapted to the grape, it must be borne in mind that neither will much avail, if resting on a subsoil of stiff clay, retentive of water. So soon as this kind of foundation is reached by the roots of the vine, mould and decay set in, and fruit and plant are doomed to certain destruction.

"The vine," Mr. Dodge observes, "has been cultivated with uniform and gratifying success in the vicinity of Wheeling, both on the hill slopes, at the top, or near the bottom, and also on the islands in the river. Low lands, especially islands, have been avoided in other localities as sites for vineyards, but a look at the islands of this vicinity will suffice to solve the mystery of their adaptedness. If subject to overflow, it is only at rare intervals of winter and spring floods, the water soon subsiding, and settling through the gravelly substratum with a rapidity almost coincident with the subsidence of the river itself. In such a soil, a great expense for trenching is an entirely unnecessary part of the labor of preparing ground for a vineyard. The Zane's Island vineyard gives, annually, a yield greater than the average yield of American vineyards. When new vines are added, the ground is broken thoroughly sixteen inches deep with three horses, then furrowed, and holes dug one foot deep in the furrows for the reception of the vines."

On the hills, however, trenches were dug in some instances, and the vines planted in holes two feet square and eighteen inches deep. This method answered very well in naturally loose, or stony soil, but in vineyards where clay was predominant, the vines, after a few years, ceased to thrive, and had to be assisted by additional trenching between the rows.

In Doddridge county a small vineyard on a good clay loam hillside, planted in holes 3 by 4 feet apart, had been in bearing six years, without ripening its fruit evenly but once or twice. A portion of it was then trenched eighteen inches deep and a marked improvement immediately resulted. Another vineyard was planted by the writer in the same vicinity, partly in holes, partly in trenches, and partly in soil thoroughly trenched eighteen inches deep, the whole on a sloping, apparently well drained bench, and the vines four feet apart in seven feet rows. But the substratum was a stiff yellow clay, which soon told upon the success of the undertaking. At the end of eight years the vines planted in holes began to wither. Two years later the part planted in trenches followed suit, but the portion thoroughly trenched would have outlived the average term, had not the mildew and rot, which affected the Catawba everywhere, induced the total abandonment of the experiment. At the same time trellice vines planted in the alluvial bottom a few feet above the level of the garden, in holes, and in loose sandy and gravelly loam, succeeded admirably, bearing and maturing to perfection the Catawba, Isabella, Concord, Black Hamburg, and Scuppernong, with but little rot, and that confined to the Catawba.

At Charleston, in the Kanawha valley, there are several trenched vineyards, planted with Catawba. The grape is subject to partial rot, and the vines drop their leaves before maturity of the fruit; but are, upon the whole, as thrifty as elsewhere in the Ohio valley.

At Washington's bottom, nine miles below Parkersburg on the Ohio river, Messrs. Munchmeyer Brothers have planted about 20 acres, of which 14 are in bearing. Their vineyard extends from the foot of the first bench or second bottom almost to the bank of the river, on a slope of not over four or five degrees, to the West. The soil is a well drained alluvial, very deep, good corn land, though not in a state of primitive fertility. The soil was ploughed 13 inches deep, and the vines planted in holes 24 inches deep, and 8 feet apart in quincunx order. The canes are trained on two laths and wires, the lowest of which is about 3 feet above the ground, and the growth of each vine strictly confined to its allotted space. These gentlemen began operations with the Catawba and Isabella, with the usual result, more or less mildew and rot after the first few years of bearing. They report but little rot in the Concord, and none in Seedling, which ripens more evenly, and to greater perfection than any vineyard grape yet seen by the writer in the Middle States. In the same vineyard there are experimental rows of Ives Seedling, Herbemont, Delaware, Iona and Muscadine, all producing perfect fruit. The latter variety is almost identical with Muscat grape of Burgundy, in flavor and appearance, and decidedly a very superior table grape.

This variety is cultivated with great care and intelligence, and highly remunerative to its owners. For the want of good cellars, very little wine is manufactured on the place, and the bulk of the crop is sold to wine making firms at Cincinnati. This year, 9 cents per pound was paid for Virginia Seedling, 7½ cents for Concord and 6 cents for Catawba and Isabella. The yield per acre for the year 1869 is estimated at 350 gallons of wine per acre.

The Concord, Virginia and Ives Seedlings have also been extensively planted near Wheeling, to replace the Catawba in process of decay, and produced several vintages, which compare very favorably with those of Ohio and Missouri. These varieties, having been planted with equal success in a great variety of soils and exposures, may be regarded as solving the problem of wine grow-

ing in West Virginia. The yield per acre is reported at 300 to 400 gallons, which brings readily, for Concord, from $1 to $1.25 per gallon, for Seedling, from $1.50 to $2 per gallon.

The object of this chapter is not to furnish a treatise on the culture of the grape, but merely to point to its condition and prospects in this State. Some pains were taken to show the difference of results among the various methods of planting, in order to meet a certain infatuation on the part of our native citizens, contemplating to engage in grape culture, who think that because the wild vine thrives and bears, shallow rooted, on any kind of land, thorough preparation of the soil is not indispensable.

Another prejudice, prevailing chiefly among European vine-dressers just across the sea, is, that close planting and pruning is not more objectionable here than in their native country. These critics entirely overlook the fact, that the American vine is of more rapid and vigorous growth, with larger joints, leaves and roots, than its European sister, and, very much like the American people, requires more room and freedom in order to prosper. As a rule, this class of workmen, who in their conceit are extremely slow to forget and to learn, should not be entrusted with the management of vineyards by owners not conversant with every branch of the business, or unable to give it their personal supervision during the most important operations.

The subject of the diseases of the grape has long been one of very elaborate investigation on the part of men of science, and Vinticultural Societies on both sides of the Atlantic, and by much ingenious research the causes were traced mainly to the close planting and pruning of the European plan. If this be correct, then the tedious and expensive remedy of sprinkling the vines with lime or sulphur may be dispensed with, and a system of culture adopted, which is summed up as follows by a very acute observer, and practical writer in the Parkersburg papers:

"Ist. In planting a vineyard, let the vines have plenty of room. For Concords, Isabellas and Catawbas, and other rampant growers, I would suggest that they be planted at least sixteen feet apart in the rows, and twelve feet between the rows, and in what is called the quincunx manner. That is, plant the first row as above, then in the second row, instead of setting the vines directly opposite to those in the first row, plant them just half-way between. In the third row plant the vines directly opposite those in the first row. In the fourth row plant the vines directly opposite those in the second row and so on, after the following diagram:

```
o   x   o   x   o   x   o   x   o   x

x   o   x   o   x   o   x   o   x   o

o   x   o   x   o   x   o   x   o   x
```

The o represents the vines and the x the posts.

2nd. Train the vines on wires, or lath are better, in the fan shape, or any other that will spread the most canes over the greatest surface, so that there will be little interference, and the light and heat of the sun will reach every leaf. Let the posts be seven feet above the ground and have from three to five wires.

3rd. Do not manure heavily with stimulating manures.

4th. Do very little summer pruning, and do that before the first of July.

6th. Thin the fruit by removing at least one-third of the bunches, provided the vine has set its full complement—i. e. an average of three bunches to the bud or eye, as soon as possible after the berries are formed.

NOTE:—Since the above was written, my attention has been called to an article in Tilton's Journal of Horticulture, for November, written by E. F. Underhill, of Brocton, N. Y., in which he takes substantially the same position as that advocated in this paper. His facts coincide with my observation in this vicinity."

The writer of the above cultivates the grape only for table use, and for that purpose 16 feet may not be too large a space for each vine. Where good wine is the object, however, 8 feet will be found sufficient, upon the universal principle that the best wine grows nearest the root.

In the absence of correct reports as to the area planted in grapes in West Virginia, no reliable statement can be made here; yet from what data the writer has been able to collect, the aggregate is not likely to exceed 400 acres, of which three-fourths are credited to the counties of Ohio and Marshall, and the remainder to the counties of Wetzel, Doddridge, Wood, Wayne, Kanawha, Cabell, Taylor, Hampshire, Jefferson and Ritchie. Upshur figures in the Census with 206 gallons of wine, and a numher of other counties with from 30 to 100 gallons each, though it is likely that in the case of the latter, the product was obtained from vines planted in gardens or trained on walls or porches. Of wild grapes, there are three or four varieties, only one of which, the Fox grape, presumed to be the ancestor of the Catawba, is worthy of notice.

TIMBER.

Among the natural elements of wealth abounding in West Virginia, none are so conspicuous, so directly available, and so evenly distributed, as her magnificent forests, which, before the ring of the woodman's axe first resounded west of the Alleghanies, shaded almost every rod of dry land of her territory. West Virginians who never had occasion to build a house, a fence, or even a chimney fire in the treeless West, or to count the cost of either operation in the older countries, are slow to realize the importance and value of the treasures in their posession. But the enterprising stranger, whose vision reaches a few years ahead, is amazed at our wanton mismanagement of this precious resource, and at our backwardness in getting it to market.

Twenty years ago, the timid remark was occasionally ventured by old residents, that our timber might *some day* become of value; but they scarcely dreamed that within a quarter of a century, West Virginia lumber would become an indispensable article of consumption and mechanical industry, not only at Pittsburgh and Cincinnati, but in the more distant marts of Baltimore, New York and New England.

DESCRIPTION OF NATIVE TIMBER.

In the absence of a standard work on American forests, and owing to the difference in popular designations of the same genera, in different States or sections of the country, it was found somewhat difficult to identify every variety under its proper botanical name. Errors or omissions that may appear in the following list will, however, be found to affect only two or three sub-varieties of minor importance.

EVERGREENS.

WHITE PINE. *Pinus Strobus.* A very large tree, when fully developed; but seldom over 120 feet high in West Virginia, and not generally prevalent. Timber equal to Pennsylvania or Michigan pine.

PITCH PINE. *Pinus rigida.* Never over 60 feet high. Thin, sandy ridges; not very abundant. Very rich in turpentine.

YELLOW PINE. *Pinus variabilis.* From 50 to 85 feet high. Tops of ridges, solitary or in small clusters. Valuable timber, not subject to warp or spring.

HEMLOCK OR HEMLOCK SPRUCE. *Pinus Canadensis.* Rich mountain and table land. From 70 to 100 feet high. Coarse grained but useful timber. Bark valuable for tanning.

BLACK SPRUCE. *Pinus nigra.* Banks of streams, and other damp places. A handsome tree, 50 to 60 feet high, of pyramidal shape in open ground. Wood not used.

RED CEDAR. *Juniperus Virginiana.* Moderate sized tree of pyramidal shape; thinly scattered through the State, disposed to come up as second growth on thin land; wood light and very durable.

HOLLY. *Ilex opaca.* Mountain streams; gravelly or sandy soil. About 15 feet high. Tough wood, good for turning purposes.

LAUREL. *Kalmia latifolia.* Thin, cold hillsides and mountains. From 4 to 10 feet high. Two varieties in West Virginia; the largest growing on Tygart's Valley river and other streams on similar elevation. Beautiful flowers; leaves poison for cattle.

DECIDUOUS TREES.

WHITE OAK. *Quercus alba*: One of the largest and most abundant trees in the State. Found in bottoms, on hillsides, and ridges. From 75 to 100 feet high, and 2½ to 4 feet in diameter. Grows in dense woods to two-thirds or three-fourths of its height, without a limb. Acorns good for mast; bears upon an average once in two years.

RED OAK. *Q. rubra.* Not quite as large as White Oak, nor as straight or durable. Bark rough and dark, valuable for tanning. Wood coarse grained but heavy. Acorns large, but inferior for mast.

BLACK OAK. *Q. tinctoria.* This is the Quercitron so valuable for its bark, the extract of which is used for dyeing and calico printing in Europe. From 40 to 80 feet high. Bark rough and blackish. Good timber; found on high benches and ridges.

JACK OAK. *Q. nigra.* Scrubby and never over 30 or 40 feet high. Not valuable. Thin sandy ridges.

SPANISH OAK. *Q. falcata.* Not very abundant. From 60 to 80 feet high. Tough and valuable; good for staves; bark valued for tanning.

CHESNUT OAK. *Q. castanea.* Abundant on rather thin and stony or clayey ridges and benches, but very thrifty in good soil also. From 60 to 80 feet high; tough and durable wood, equal to White Oak for many purposes; furnishes a larger supply of tan bark than any other oak. Known as Yellow Oak in other countries.

In addition to the above, one or two varieties of scrub oak are sometimes met with, especially among evergreen timber in the mountains, but not well defined.

POPLAR, properly TULIP TREE. *Liliodendron Tulipifera.* White and Yellow Poplar; the latter the most valuable for flooring, ceiling and cabinet work, also for shingles; answers all the purposes of pine. This is the largest tree in West Virginia, attaining a height of from 100 to 150 feet and a corresponding diameter. Flourishes equally well in the valleys, and on rich hillsides and ridges. In the East, paper has been manufactured from the bark, which is also an excellent tonic, used in the manufacture of bitters.

BLACK WALNUT. *Juglans nigra.* From 50 to 80 feet high and from 3 to 6 feet in diameter. In open ground grows large limbs, widely spread. Found in rich soil at any elevation, but nowhere so abundant as in some of the mountain sections. Nut of fine quality.

WHITE WALNUT, (Butternut.) *Juglans cinerea.* Grows nearly as large as the black walnut, and multiplies more rapidly. Bark used for dyeing home made woolens. Inner bark yields a laxative extract. Nut of softer shell than black walnut.

HICKORY. *Carya Sulcata.* Thick shell bark hickory.

SHELL BARK, or SHAG BARK HICKORY. *Carya alba.* Both varieties abundant in rich soil among deciduous timber, the bark of the latter separating more freely and fruit with a thinner shell. Height from 80 to 100 feet, diameter seldom over 2½ to 3 feet, grain fine, fibre hard and flexible. The best fuel in our woods.

WHITE HEART HICKORY. *C. tomentosa.* Similar to the above, but white to the core, and superior for uses requiring strength and flexibility. Bark rough but not scaly.

BROOM HICKORY, (Pignut.) *C. porcina.* Similar to above with a very tough fibre. Best for splint brooms. Fruit small and bitter.

CHESNUT. *Castanea vesca Am.* A large and spreading tree. Dry, elevated ground in every part of the State, but more abundant in the mountains. Rapid growth; may be renewed from the sprout or seed every 15 or 20 years to sufficient size for splitting posts and rails. Wood very strong and durable, next to locust for posts. Fruit of superior quality.

CHINQUAPIN. *C. pumila.* A small tree, not abundant. Small edible fruit.

BUCKEYE, or HORSE CHESNUT. *Aesculus glabra.* Large tree of rapid growth; prefers bottom land. Soft wood, not durable when exposed. Bears fruit very young, not edible.

LOCUST. *Robinia Pseudaccacia.* Good sized tree, in thin or open woods on high ground. Irregularly distributed, generally found in groves; a rapid grower and easily propagated.

HONEY LOCUST. *Gleditschia triacantos.* Moderate size, thorny. Very fragrant flower; not abundant.

BEECH. *Fagus sylvatcia.* White and red. Found in bottoms and on lower, benches all over the State, moderately abundant. Height 50 or 60 feet; not much used yet, except for fuel. Good for boxes, journals in machinery, chair bottoms, and makes durable fence boards when nailed up and exposed to the air immediately after being sawed. Nut very sweet and fattening.

SYCAMORE. *Platanus occidentalis.* A very large and picturesque tree from 70 to 120 feet high; solitary, or in beautiful clusters along the banks of streams; white smooth bark, very fine, hard wood, used for bedsteads and other turned furniture; rapid grower and easily propagated.

ELM. *Ulmus Americana.* A very handsome spreading tree from 60 to 80 feet high, seldom found in the woods, most frequently on river banks and more or less open ground. Seldom cut down for any purpose.

CUCUMBER. *Magnolia accuminata.* Moderate sized tree, seldom more than 70 feet high, white wood, not very hard or fibrous, and very manageable under the turning lathe. Germans use it for *wooden shoes*, and other hollow ware; bark aromatic, large showy flower; fruit resembles a small cucumber, and is taken along by Virginians going West, as an antidote and remedy for fever and ague.

LINDEN, or LIMETREE, (vulg. Basswood or Linn.) *Tilia.* Rich soil, height 60 to 80 feet, soft white wood, well adapted to light cabinet work. Easily reduced to a pulp and suitable for paper manufacturing; sweet scented flowers; bark makes ropes for temporary purposes.

WHITE ASH. *Fraxinus Americana.* A large, straight tree, on rich hillsides; wood tough and elastic, used for flooring, mill works and carriages; much sought after.

MOUNTAIN ASH. *Pyrus Americana.* Not over 40 feet high; said to occur in the mountains, not well identified.

WILD CHERRY. *Cerasus crotina.* A fine looking tree from 40 to 70 feet high, diameter from 2 to 6 and even 7 feet; not very abundant, nor of the largest size, except on the table lands immediately below the Alleghany summits; fine grained, valuable wood; fruit made into brandy and *bounce*; bark and twigs highly medicinal.

MAPLE, (Hard Maple or Sugartree.) *Acer Saccharinum.* A beautiful tree, growing on rich ground to a height of 80 feet. Wood bright, finely curled, tough and compact; used for many mechanical purposes; first class, but expensive fuel. Abundant all over the State, especially in the mountain counties, where, in several sections it constitutes one-half of the timber. The fall hue of the leaves is the brightest red in American landscape.

BLACK SUGAR MAPLE. *Acer nigrum.* Resembles the above somewhat in foliage, but has a darker bark and darker, coarse wood; yields a saccharine sap, but is not developed where the preceeding variety prevails.

GUM. *Liquidamber.* (Sweet Gum.) A tall slender tree, not often very straight; with twisty wood that cannot be split, used for mill works and carriage hubs; resists fire longer than any timber in the country.

SOUR GUM, (Black Gum.) *Nyssa multiflora.* From 50 to 60 feet high; bottom lands; wood tough and twisty as in preceeding variety.

BIRCH. *Betula.* White, Red, and Sweet or Cherry Birch are represented in various parts of the State. The writer has seen more of them on Elk river and tributaries, and on table lands than elsewhere; height from 40 to 70 feet. A graceful, picturesque tree, especially on river banks; the wood of the Yellow Birch alone is said to be valuable for cabinet work and its bark is used by tanners in other States.

ALDER. *Alnus serrulata.* From 10 to 15 feet high, on river banks.

WATER BEECH. (Hornbeam.) *Carpinus Am.* From 18 to 20 feet high; on banks of streams, rough, intricate branches, tough wood, but not used.

IRONWOOD. *Ostrya Virginica.* 30 to 40 feet high; heavier and even tougher than hickory, unsurpassed as a lever.

ASPEN. *Populus pendula* (?). A rare tree, not properly identified in West Virginia, but evidently belonging to the poplar family. Specimens seen as high as 50 or 60 feet in the central counties. Another variety of young trees were found in Doddridge county, much resembling the Silverleaved Poplar.

Of the smaller and less important varieties of timber and brushwood, the following most conspicuous may be added to the list:

Mulberry, Persimmon, Hazelnut, Pawpaw, Crab-apple, Wild Plum, Hawthorn, Service, Wild Grape, and Elder, all of which are fruit-bearing and numerously represented. Then we have: Leatherwood, Dogwood, good for handspikes, wedges, &c., Sassafras, Slippery Elm, Spicewood, Witch Hazel, several varieties of Willows, one of which good for basket work, Sumach, Red Bud, Pipestem, Honeysuckle, &c.

A volume, larger than this Handbook, could be filled with a brief description of the endless array of shrubs, roots, barks, plants and herbs used in industrial arts and pharmacy, not omitting the Rattleweed or Snakeroot, and last, but not least, that famous back county staple, Ginseng, of which many tons are still being gathered and exported to China, for medical purposes not fully appreciated upon its own native soil.

If the medical works of the Thompsonian school are to be believed, West Virginia possesses in her fields, forests and mountains, an inexhaustible supply of unfailing remedies for all and every ill the human family is heir to, in every country on the face of the globe.

WASTE AND VALUE OF TIMBER.

The exportation of sawlogs, shiptimber, lumber, staves and barrels from West Virginia, now computed at $2,500,000 per annum, must assume enormous proportions as the natural supply of surrounding States diminishes, and our own shipping facilities are increased. The clearing of timbered land in the United States, for agricultural and manufacturing purposes, is reported at 3,000,000 acres per annum, or 10,000 acres, for each working day. In the six or seven principal lumber States the production has been annually decreasing for several years past. In New York 200,000 acres of timbered land is cleared away annually; in Ohio not less than 100,000. Our neighbor State, Maryland, with the exception of one county, already severely culled, has little, or no wood land left. In Eastern Virginia, where good timber has been getting scarce for years, the destruction of buildings, fences, railroad bridges and cross ties, during the war, has been immense, and is not yet retrieved. In Pennsylvania, the lumber trade has denuded entire district that once seemed inexhaustible, and development is now confined to the rougher and least accessible sections. Those of the lumber men who shun the hardships of the new fields, are transferring their capital and enterprise to the more inviting regions of West Virginia.

When it is considered that three-fourths of the land, now being cleared, will be permanently diverted from the production of timber, and that even if permitted to grow up again, will require two or three centuries to replace a tree, the lumber from which may last but a few years; that the ratio of increase in the consumption of lumber is nearly double that of the increase in population; that the Census reports 36 occupations, representating 475,000 artisans and laborers in the United States engaged in the manufacture of articles of commerce and consumption from wood; and that every article so produced, from a shingle to a railroad bridge, and from a clothes pin to an ocean steamer, is of a perishable nature, and must be renewed every few years; when all this is considered, it appears that the price of lumber must increase from 25 to 50 per cent. every ten years, as it has done for the last decade or two, and that it will become a question, even in the back counties of West Virginia, whether it is more profitable to destroy timber now, to make room for the production of bread and meat, or to hold it a few years longer for ready cash.

CAPACITY AND PROSPECTS.

Of the 16,640,000 acres constituting the area of West Virginia, 14,000,000 acres, or nearly seven-eights are unimproved, and of these at least 10,000,000 acres are still in all the vigor and freshness of original growth. Reserving 4,000,000 acres for all the purposes of home consumption, which under economical management is abundantly sufficient for the domestic purposes of a population of two millions, in a country so rich in coal, there remain 6,000,000 acres, averaging at a low estimate 5000 feet of lumber per acre, which at the customary rate of $2.50 per thousand, on the stump, gives

$12.50 per acre, or $75,000,000, and at the average price of $16 per thousand, for lumber manufactured, sawed and delivered at the railroad or river stations, represent an aggregate value of ($480,000,000) four hundred and eighty millions of dollars!

Michigan statistics exhibit that State under process of being denuded of 1,500,000,000 feet of lumber per annum, valued at $21,000,000 dollars. At this rate it is estimated that she cannot keep up the supply longer than 15 years, without stinting her own population. And a similar result is inevitable in West Virginia. When our contemplated railroads and river improvements will be constructed, and the exportation of lumber from West Virginia gradually increases, until the average annual amount will be three or four times what it now is, we shall have less than half a century to run through with our spare timber. Before the end of that time we will have to engage in planting, to provide for future generations, under penalty of paying four times as much for timber from British America, or the Amazon region, than we received for our own.

A moderate amount of figuring over statistical data will show that there is no exaggeration whatever in this estimate, which should warn us of the necessity of entering at once upon a more economical management of a resource, about the value of which we appear to be entirely at sea.

In small and widely scattered clearings, remote from market and transportation facilities, the waste of timber will be inevitable yet for years to come; but in denser settlements, accessible to light, portable sawmills, hundreds and thousands could be annually saved from the log heap, with little extra labor. And even without a mill, staves, shingles, wagon stuff, shipknees, and even blocks for veneering could be hewed, sawed by hand, split and riven out of oak, poplar, hickory, chesnut, walnut and ash, and stored away under shelter, until the improvement of the surrounding country opens a local demand or a way to market.

The time will come when even railroad ties will attain a sufficient price to justify storing up, or hauling on wheels for several miles. Each mile of railroad requires 2000 sleepers or crossties, to be renewed every seven years. At this rate the Baltimore & Ohio R. R. Wheeling and Parkersburg branches alone, consume 166,571 ties per annum, representing, at 40 cents per stick, a value of nearly $70,000, mainly furnished by West Virginia, and requiring to be hauled to the track over a greater distance each succeeding year.

MEANS OF TRANSPORTATION.

The lumber trade in West Virginia has been among the earliest vocations of the pioneers who settled on the banks of navigable or "raftable" streams. In the absence of anything like a reliable record of the business, some idea of its extent may be formed from the fact, that streams like the Little Kanawha, Guyandotte and Big Sandy rivers respectively, bring down logs in rafts to the aggregate value of from $40,000 to $50,000 at a single rise. Up to this date, rafting and floating have been confined to the larger streams and tributaries, yet the floating of single logs and small rafts is practicable from five to six miles below the source of almost any stream West of a line of rapids, extending from the Valley Falls in Taylor county, to the Kentucky line, and crossing Elk river 8 or 10 miles above the mouth of Holly, the Little Kanawha at Bulltown, and the Great Kanawha at the Great Falls in the county of Fayette. East of that line, the rapidity and tortuousness of the streams and protruding rocks and boulders in their beds interfere, more or less, with the safety of rafts, though single logs are floated down without much trouble, and then caught and rafted in the stiller water below.

Not only timber in the log, but staves and sawed lumber, green and seasoned, are floated down the principal streams in good sized boats. From counties as far inland as Lewis, Gilmer, Braxton, Calhoun, Roane, Nicholas, Fayette, Raleigh, Wyoming and McDowell, and the counties below these, boats, with gunwales hewn out from a single poplar, over 100 feet in length are brought down in ordinary freshets without difficulty. Smaller sized boats descend Fishing Creek, Middle Island and Sand Creeks from points within 10 miles of their uppermost source.

As late as ten years ago, seven-eighths of the lumber consumed in the State and exported, were manufactured by water-power; but since then, portable and stationary steam sawmills have rapidly increased. Along both branches of the Baltimore & Ohio R. R., from twenty to thirty first class mills, are cutting on an average 3000 feet per day. This product consists of flooring, scantling, furniture stuff and ship and railroad timber, for Eastern and Western markets, the Railroad Company itself being an important customer. Many of these mills possess a capacity of 10,000 feet of lumber per day, which maximum is seldom reached for want of adequate force to supply logs, and take care of the lumber. Large mills are also in operation at the principal points on the Ohio and its largest West Virginia tributaries. A company of enterprising Pennsylvanians, with a capital of $300,000, under the corporate style of "The Elk River Land, Improvement, Manufacturing and Boom Company," obtained a charter for the exclusive privilege of booming Elk river and tributaries, as far up as the mouth of Holly river, and are now engaged in developing 80,000 acres of land in Braxton and Webster counties with sawmills, planing mills and business headquarters at Charleston, on the Great Kanawha. One of the first operations of this Company was the shipping by river to Parkersburg, and thence by rail to Baltimore, of 10,000 feet black walnut plank, which, notwithstanding expensive freight over a distance of 650 miles, yielded a handsome profit.

KINDS AND LOCALITIES OF TIMBER.

The largest proportion of West Virginia timber now being developed, consists of Oak and Poplar, found everywhere in the State, except on a few high levels in the mountain section. Walnut, Cherry, Sycamore, Ash, Chesnut, Chesnut Oak and Locust are next in importance, though much less abundant. In the whole basin drained by Fishing Creek, Middle Island Creek, Little Kanawha and branches, Sand Creek, Great Kanawha and those of its branches emptying into it below the Falls; and then Guyandotte and Big Sandy rivers, these species of timber attain a size not surpassed on the North American continent east of the Rocky Mountains. Here, straight and stalwart oaks and hickorys, and poplars may be found, towering up side by side, interlacing their contracted crowns 75 or 100 feet above the ground, representing to the business man from 800 to 1500 feet of lumber per tree, and to the lover of the grand and beautiful in nature, some of the most imposing sylvan scenes imaginable. This region is emphatically the home of deciduous timber; but evergreens, especially the white pine, are seldom met here, except in occasional groves, and scarcely ever of the largest size, or unmixed with other timber.

East of the line of rapids mentioned above, evergreens gradually increase in size and quantity, and the largest pine region in the State probably extends through the counties of Fayette and Raleigh, on both sides of New river and some distance up Gauley river. In the mountain counties, not only the White Pine, but the Hemlock and Spruce are extensively found among deciduous timber, and of remarkable size and faultless growth. The finest specimens of Hemlock abound in the Cheat and Greenbrier mountains, and on the table lands of Tucker, Randolph, Pendleton, Pocahontas, Nicholas and Webster. Here also, as mentioned in the chapter on climate, neither Oak, Poplar or Hickory are to be found, but in their room thrive noble specimens of Sugar or Hard Maple, Ash, Beech, Birch, Wild Cherry and Black Walnut, some of the two latter measuring from 4 to 5 feet, and exceptionally even 6 or 7 feet in diameter. From the Staunton and Parkersburg turnpike, near the head of Greenbrier river, toward the north, south and east, stretch upward of 150,000 acres of the most magnificent forest in the State, scarcely broken by less than fifty scattered mountain farms. These lands, which may now be purchased at $1.25 to $2 per acre, will easily command from $5 to $10 per acre so soon as an outlet for timber is provided.

When land is cleared in this region, the beech, ash and even the sugar are girdled, and burned or permitted to decay upon the ground, and *Virginia worm fences* are built of Black Walnut and Wild Cherry, worth in Baltimore from $45 to $80 per thousand feet. There is no remedy for this, almost criminal waste, except in the speedy construction of an outlet to the nearest navigable point of Cheat river, at, or near Tucker Court House, a distance of 25 miles above Rowlesburg station, on the Baltimore & Ohio R. R. From the Staunton turnpike to Tucker Court House, or St. George, the distance is about 55 miles by way of the Laurel Fork of Cheat river, and a double track tram road connecting those two points, would promote the development of a region large enough for a separate county, and unsurpassed in timbered wealth, and grazing and dairy facilities. Above the main forks of Cheat, in Tucker county, the several branches of the river are entirely too rough and too rapid for safe navigation, though it is supposed that with some blasting, Laurel Fork could be made practical for single logs and small rafts.

Main Cheat river, for some 20 or 25 miles above the railroad and the Black Fork of Cheat, have been to some extent developed 15 years ago for ship timber, for the English market, by a company whose mill-works were located at Rowlesburg. This whole Cheat river region also abounds in valuable tanbark which is largely consumed by extensive tanneries in the vicinity, or shipped East even as far as Europe. The Black Oak, or Quercitron, is also present here, and in fact elsewhere in the State, in sufficient numbers to justify development, and although the bark commands $10 per cord East, no one has yet thought of turning it to account.

The white oak timber from the foot of the Cheat mountains to the Ohio river, in the railroad counties of Preston, Taylor, Harrison, Doddridge, Ritchie and Wood grows chiefly on heavy, but rich clay loam, holding more or less iron and potash, and is estimated of very superior quality and durability. For oil barrels, requiring a close, impermeable grain, it is not excelled anywhere. Several factories along the road are turning out from 150 to 200 barrels per day, besides shipping immense quantities of dressed and seasoned staves for coopering at Baltimore, and as far North as Massachusetts.

Along the line of railroad, well timbered land is sold at from $10 to $16 per acre, and several operators have obtained their timber clear of cost, by fencing and cleaning off the smoothest portions of their lands after sawing up all the available timber, and then selling the whole at original cost. This operation will be found practicable in any nook and corner of the State to which a steam sawmill may be conveyed.

Staves are now being made almost at the very source of the streams flowing toward the railroad and Ohio river, floated down loosely in time of freshets, and caught by booms at convenient points. Good white oak staves, 34 inches long, 1 inch thick at the heart edge, command now from $18 to $20 per thousand along the railroad. For larger or smaller staves, the owners of the land or timber pay from $7.50 to $8.00 per thousand for making and piling them up at a place in the woods accessible to teams, so that from $8 to $10 per thousand remains for timber, transportation and profit. Dry staves are now being hauled to the Baltimore barrel factory at Pennsboro, by wagon, from 12 to 15 miles over indifferent roads, and still leave an encouraging profit to the producer.

The development of ship timber is receiving much attention just now along the railroad, and late orders from abroad have disclosed the fact, that not only oak, but other kinds of West Virginia timber were in demand for that purpose, as for instance :

White Oak, for keels, planking, beams, knees, floors and ceilings.

Ash, for blocks, oars, &c.

Hickory, for capstan bars and handspikes.

Sugar or Hard Maple, for keels or bottom plank.

Beech, red preferred, for frames, planking &c.

Poplar, for cabinet work.

White Oak knees bring higher prices in proportion to cost than any other class of ship timber, and will amply repay hauling on country roads to the station over 15 or 20 miles. Thousands of limbs and tops, admirably shaped for knees, are thoughtlessly destroyed in our clearings every year.

Hoop poles are among the primitive commodities exported from West Virginia, and, being speedily renewed from the root or stump, the supply is almost inexhaustible, so long as the grubbing hoe is kept out of the woods. The home price for a good article of hickory or white oak is from $8 to $10 per thousand.

Wagon and carriage stuff is beginning to be manufactured for exportation at various points of the railroad. The prejudice heretofore prevailing in favor of Connecticut hickory is rapidly waning, judging from the large orders now being received for West Virginia spokes, etc. An occasional survey of the railroad depot at Parkersburg, when filled with tons of wagons, carriages, ploughbeams, furniture and twenty other articles of wooden ware, manufactured from West Virginia timber, *outside of the State*, and westward bound, gives but a faint idea of what is continually being lost through our lack of manufacturing enterprise. What a difference would be realized in amount of our production and consequent prosperity, if to the bare value of timber exported in the log, we could add from 300 to 500 per cent. as the price of mechanical skill and labor, earned, and consumed or permanently invested here by our own population?

PRICE OF LOGS, LUMBER, &c.

The following prices are now being paid for timber in the log, per cubic foot, at Parkersburg, Guyandotte and other points along the Ohio river:

Pine, one cube	9@10	cents,	two	cube	11@12	cents
Poplar, "	"	8@10	"	"	"	10@12	"
Oak, "	"	9@10	"	"	"	18	"
Walnut,	"	10@12	"	"	"	15@18	"
Cherry,	"	10@12	"	"	"	15@18	"
Ash, "	"	8@10	"	"	"	10@12	"

Sawed lumber at the above named points and stations of the Baltimore & Ohio R. R. is commanding at present, per thousand feet: Poplar $15 to 16; Oak $18 to 20; Walnut and Cherry $30 to 35; White Oak staves 33 inch. long, 1 inch thick at heart edge $18 to 20—¾ inch thick $15 to 18; Poplar, Oak and Chesnut shingles, sawed, $4 50 per thousand.

Wholesale Lumber Prices at Baltimore.

Poplar and White Oak inch flooring plank	$26a28
Black Walnut, (West Virginia) 5-8 to 2 inch. thick	55a70
Cherry plank, inch. thick	38a45
White Oak Staves, 33 in. long 4 to 5 in. wide, 1½ in. thick per M	38a40
“ “ “ “ , 4 to 6 in. “ 1¾ “ “	42a45
Heading, 32 in. long, 8 to 12 in. wide, 1½ “ “	48
Light Hhd. Staves, 45 in. long, 4 to 5 in. wide, ¾ to 1 in. thick, per M	50a53
Heavy “ “ 44 in. long 4½ to 6 in. wide, 1½ in. thick, “	55a60
Light Pipe Staves, 56 in. long. 4 to 6 in. wide, 1¾ in. thick, “	55a60
Heavy “ “ 57 in. long, 5 to 7 in. wide, 1¾ in. thick, “	90o75
Hoop Poles. for whiskey bbls. shaved, 9 feet long, per M	13a14
do for flour bbls. Oak or Hickory, per M	10a13
do for Hhds. “ “ shaved, per M.	20a25
Bark, Black Oak, (quercitron) per cord	9a10
do Black Oak, (rossed quercitron) per ton	14a15
do Chesnut Oak, per cord	16
do Sumac, bark and twigs, per ton	65

Wholesale Lumber Prices at Cincinnati.

Poplar, dry inch plank per M	$25a28
Oak “ “ “	25a28
Pine, “ clear, first quality, per M	55a60
do “ first common, “	45n50
do “ second do “	30a33
Poplar, green, on arrival, per M	20
Oak, “ “ “	18a20
Ash, “ “ “	22a24
Walnut, “ “ “	40a45
Cherry, “ “ “	30a35

Cincinnati prices for staves of every description generally range from 25 to 30 per cent. below Baltimore prices, but the difference is compensated by the lower rates of river freight.

Wholesale Lumber Prices at Pittsburg.

Oak, Poplar, Ash, Walnut, and Cherry average from 10 to 15 per cent higher than at Cincinnati.

Oil barrel staves 33 to 34 inch. long and 1 inch at the heart side $27a30.

Pittsburg is the best market for lumber, staves, &c., shipped by Railroad from any point west of Grafton.

The freight rates to Baltimore do not allow any profit on green lumber, and dry lumber and staves pay best in either market.

Locust Timber, in rough, Price at Parkersburg.

Locust Pins, 14 in. long by 1¾ square, full size, per M	$10
do 16 “ “ “ “ “	10
do 18 “ “ “ “ “	10
do 20 “ “ “ “ “	10
do 22 “ “ “ “ “	10
do 22 “ 1½ “ “ “	12

Freight Tariff of the Baltimore & Ohio R. R. Co., for Logs, Timber and Plank, no more than 30 feet long, Hoop Poles, Staves, &c., in full car loads, carried at the following rates.

To Baltimore.	Number of miles.	Rate of fr'ght per ton of 2000 pounds..	To Baltimore.	Number of miles.	Rate of fr'ght per ton of 2000 pounds..
			Burton	330	$6.85
MAIN STEM.					
Harper's Ferry	81	$2.90	Cameron	351	7.00
Martinsburg	100	3.90	Moundsville	368	7.00
Great Cacapon	131	4.30	Benwood	375	7.00
Patterson Creek	170	4.70	Wheeling	379	7.00
Cumberland	178	4.90	PARKERSBURG BR'H.		
New Creek	201	5.05	Webster	283	6.25
Piedmont	206	5.05	Flemmington	289	6.40
Swanton	220	5.10	Bridgeport	296	6.50
Oakland	232	5.30	Clarksburg	301	6.60
Cranberry Summit.	242	5.40	Wilsonburg	305	6.60
Rowlesburg	253	5.65	Salem	315	6.70
Tunnelton	260	5.85	West Union	329	6.80
Independence	269	6.10	Pennsboro	341	6.90
Grafton	279	6.20	Ellenboro	346	7.00
Valley River Falls.	187	6.25	Cornwallis	351	7.00
Fairmont	302	6.60	Kanawha	376	7.00
Mannington	319	6.70	Parkersburg	383	7.00

Lumber, &c., Westward from Baltimore, or from Way to Way stations Westward, the charge will be made at 15 per cent. advance upon the above rates for same distance to Baltimore.

Between Way Stations the charge Eastwardly will be made at 10 per cent. advance on that for the same distance to Baltimore.

This trade will be accommodated, in all cases when practicable, by Gondola cars, and the car load will be rated at not less than 20,000 pounds, or 10 tons at the above charges. Pins, Staves, &c., requiring House Cars, must pay not less than 18,000 pounds, or 8 tons at the above rates.

No car load for any distance, however short, shall pay less than five dollars.

The cars to be weighed in all cases, when going to, or passing stations with car scales, otherwise the weight will be estimated according to the following, viz:

Firewood and Posts and Rails, if dry, at 4,000 or if green, at from 5,000 to 5,500 lbs. per cord. Pine and Hemlock Board, Plank and Scantling, if well seasoned, at 2500 lbs. and if not well seasoned, at 3,000 lbs. per M. feet B. M. Ash, Oak, Walnut, Maple and Cherry, if dry, 3,500 lbs., if not dry, 4,500 to 6,000 lbs. per M. feet B. M. Green Whitewood Boards 4,000 lbs. per M. feet B. M.

MINERAL RESOURCES.

The information contained under this head would be more authentic and complete, if based upon a thorough geological survey of the State. Such a measure was first proposed by the writer, when a member of the Legislature, in 1864, but postponed then and ever since upon the plea, that the Treasury of the new State was absorbed by public enterprises of more urgent necessity.

Up to date the highest authority generally cited upon the subject of West Virginia minerals, is the Report of Prof. H. D. Rogers, who from 1836 to 1840 conducted the geological survey of the State of Virginia, which was never completed. Prof. Roger's investigations, so far as they extended, were very thorough and reliable, but at this time his valuable Reports cannot be procured in the original, the last official copy having strayed from the public library at Richmond two years ago.

COAL.

The area of coal in West Virginia is computed at 15,000 sq. miles, after making a liberal deduction for so much of the coal measures as was carried off by the erosion of the valleys, no allowance being made for seams dipping under the water level in the higher sections of the State, and possibly in some of the others. The coal measures are known to embrace the entire State, with the exception of the lower Potomac counties, and the strata, with few exceptions, running nearly horizontally or with but slight undulations, through the whole of this territory, there is scarcely a county within its bounds, that does not contain one or more seams, at some distance above or below the water level. Only three States of the Union outrank West Virginia in the area of coal, namely: Illinois, total area, 30,000 square miles; Iowa 24,000, and Missouri 21,000. West Virginia exceeds Pennsyvania 1,000 square miles, and contains one-thirteenth of the coal area of the whole

United States, by surface measure only, no account being taken of her greater aggregate thickness of workable seams.

The late Prof. R. C. Taylor, a learned and skillful geologist and mining engineer in the Pennsyvania coal regions, also visited some of the richest coal districts of West Virginia, but the following statements in his interesting work, (Statistics of Coal) appears to be principally taken from Prof. Roger's Report:

"At Wheeling, and for fourteen miles down the Ohio, the cliff or bank of the river presents an uninterrupted bed of highly bituminous coal, about ten feet thick. This seam, with some smaller ones, constitute Wm. B. Roger's "upper coal series," and extends from Pittsburg southward to Clarksburg, in the parallel of Marietta; and according to Prof. H. D. Rogers does not extend beyond the Guyandotte river.

Along the valley of Monongahela are several fine beds of coal. One of them, distinguished as the Pittsburgh seam, is the ten foot bed spoken of, which, to some is known by the name of the "Main Coal" of Northern Virginia, and is readily recognized where it passes the Great and Little Kanuwha rivers, and thence to the Big Sandy river on the borders of Kentucky.

The greatest thickness of workable coal is stated to be nine and a half feet at the mouth of the Scott's run, a third is from three or four feet. A fourth, geologically the highest known coal bed of any value in Virginia, Pennsylvania and Ohio, is five feet in thickness.

The workable coal seams in the upper group, are thus enumerated by the State geologist:

The first, or main seam from	5 to 9	feet.
The second,	3½	"
The third	5½	"
The fourth	7	"
Total	25	

Twenty-five feet workable, and one vein not workable. Besides beds of limestone amounting to fifty-feet thick.

The middle division or group contains five feet of coal in three beds, and twenty-four feet of limestone, in eleven beds.

The lower group contains five small seams, whose aggregate is but nine feet, only one bed of which is workable.

It would seem, therefore, that these thirteen coal beds, having an agggregate thickness of forty feet, four seams, comprisng eight yards of workable coal through nearly the whole length of the State, may be relied upon as the productive power of Western Virginia."

Mr. Taylor gives a table of analysis of European and Amercan coals from which the following, referring to West Virginia, also taken from Prof. Roger's Report, are selected:

County.	Locality.	Designation of coal beds.	Analysis.		
			Car-bon.	Vola-tile m'tt'r	Ash-es.
Harrison.........	Clarksburg.....	Main seam......	56.74	41.66	1.60
Taylor............	Pruntytown...	"	57.60	39.00	3.40
Monongalia....	Morgantown...	"	60.54	37.30	2.14
Kanawha........	Coal Creek......	Turner's Bank	55.55	41.85	2.60
"	Grand Creek...	"	52·75	43.20	4.05
Logan............	Guyandotte.....	"	56.50	42.00	1.50
"	Big Sandy......	Traa Fork......	55.00	41.00	4.00
Fayette...........		Pigeon Creek..	80.24	17.48	2.28
"	B. Sewell M'n.	L. Sewell M'n.	75.88	22.32	1.80
"	Second seam...	Roger's seam..	74.55	21.13	4.32
Kanawha........	Campbell's C...	Stockton's m'e	55.76	32.54	11.80
"	"	Ruffner's 2 s'm	64.16	32.24	3.60
"	"	Noyes seam....	65,64	31.18	3.08
"	Hughe's Bank	"	62.32	32.88	4.80
"	D. Ruffner's B	"	57.28	35.08	7.64
Mineral..........	Brantsburg.....	Upper seam....	72.40	19.72	7.88
"	Oliver's Tract..	Above m. Sav.	79.08	16.28	5.64
Grant..............	F. of Stony R'r	12 foot seam....	79.16	15.52	5.32
"	Abraham's C...	Lower seam....	72.40	15.20	12.40
"	Stony River....	Michael's........	83.36	13.28	3·36
"	Michael's........	N. of Turnpike	45.24	14.96	39.80
Preston...........	Kingwood......	Upperport.......	73,68	21.00	5.22
"	Cheat r. n. K'd	Foman Basin..	60.36	25.00	14.64
"	Kingwood.......	Price's............	68.32	26.48	5.20
"	"	Hogan's.........	67.28	29.68	3.04

The most rĕcent mineral exploration of West Virginia was made a few years ago by Prof. Harries S. Daddow, geologist and mining engineer, of Pottsville, Pennsylvania, and is thus given in his practical and exhaustive book, "Coal, Iron and Oil" page 338—342.

"West Virginia contains a larger portion of the Alleghany coal-field than any of the States enumerated through which it extends. Over 16,000 square miles of this great coal-field lie in Western and Eastern Virginia: of this area, however, only a few miles exist in Old Virginia, on the eastern edge of the field in the southwest,—perhaps less than 150 square miles of available coal. But the best and most available portion of the Alleghany coal-field lies in West Virginia, and the greater portion of its vast area is naturally opened to development by the numerous streams which traverse its face from east to west.

The Great Kanawha River, running off at right angles from the Ohio, traverse the richest portions of the Great Alleghany coal-fields, cutting the coal measures of this region—2000 feet thick—to their base, and developing their exhaustless mineral treasures in the most available manner for practical production. But, after performing this most acceptable service to the future prosperity of the West, it renders the benefits conferred still more valuable, by dividing the otherwise impassable Appalachian chain at right angles, and taking the *nearest course* to the waters of the East, thus opening the most available route from the great rivers of the West to the seaports of the East, and connecting the minerals of the older geological formations—the iron, lead copper, &c.—with the coal of the Alleghany.

The Kanawha region is still undeveloped, and the prize long sought after by the dilatory Virginian slave-master is still to be accomplished by the enterprise of free labor. In no other portion of our country, North or South, are there more inviting prospects to labor, enterprise, and capital than is now presented in the Great Kanawha Valley. Not only its unlimited mineral resources invite attention, but the best portion of the trade of the great Mississippi Valley may be diverted into the channel of the Kanawha by ordinary means. To those who have observed the prodigious growth of that trade, and the still superior proportion it must assume in the future, the questions we are discussing of this new route to the East will not be a matter of speculation, but of necessity. The routes now provided will not accommodate it, while the superior advantages offered by this route, in the hands of a free and enterprising people cannot fail to attract attention. The *distance*, the *elevation*, the freedom from *ice*, and the constant supply of *water* from the mouth of the Kanawha, all present important and available advantages which cannot be overlooked.

DISTANCES FROM EAST TO WEST.

It will be noticed, by table distances given below, that the distance from the head of navigation on the Kanawha to the head of navigation on the James river, at Richmond, is 320 miles,—or thirty-six miles less by land than from Pittsburg to Philadelphia; with a saving in distance by water from Cincinnati, as a center, of 200 miles. It is also sixty-three miles less by rail than the distance from Parkersburg to Baltimore, with about the same distance by water.

Table of Distances.

	Miles.
Charleston to New Orleans, by water	1847
Charleston to Cincinnati, "	269
Charleston to Point Pleasant, "	60
Charleston to Parkersburg, "	132
Charleston to Pittsburg, "	315
Charleston to Philadelphia *via* Pittsburg	617
Charleston to Baltimore *via* Parkersburg	515
Charleston to Richmond, Va., *via* Covington & Ohio R. R.	320
Charleston to Richmond, Va., *via* " Central "	351
Cincinnati to Philadelphia *via* Pittsburg	816
Cincinnati to Baltimore *via* Parkersburg	671
Cincinnati to Richmond *via* Charleston and Covington	589
Cincinnati to Richmond *via* Charleston and Central	610

THE COALS OF THE GREAT KANAWHA REGION

As we shall specially describe, are of various constituencies, and are adaptable to all the requirements of the trades and manufactures. The *hard* and *caking*, with the fat and gaseous bituminous, the variable splint, and the rich and oily cannel, are all found in the same mountains, and are all accessible to the miner and to navigation, through the agencies of the eroding waters, which have exposed coal in a thousand places.

The avenues to markets afford the cheapest and most available transportation on navigable rivers; while the markets themselves are unlimited in extent, and rapidly increasing their consumption.

The whole valley of the Mississippi is open beyond controlling competition to the trade and the production of this region, while the present avenues to the East and the commerce of the world are but little less available than from the older and more developed centres, with *this* advantage ever open to the Kanawha region,—that a route may be constructed having every advantage over the most favorable avenues of the trade now open from the East to the West.

This is, therefore, the *natural mining* and *manufacturing center* not only of West Virginia, but of the Great Alleghany coal-field; and had the Virginians any share of free enterprise and energy, Charleston would long ago have been a formidable rival to Pittsburg.

Looking to the natural results of location and availability, now that this magnificent region is open to free labor and a corresponding development, we may anticipate for Charleston the dignity of the State capital at no very distant day, or, what may be better, the metropolis of the mining and manufacturing interests of the West.

Coal River, Elk River, and Gauley diverge from the Great Kanawha and spread their branches over one of the richest and most magnificent coal regions in the world, and bring down their wealth to one common center on the Great Kanawha; or such might and may be the result under future developments.

The coals of this region, generally, are better, purer and more available for all the requirements of trade and manufacture than the coals of any other portion of the Alleghany coal-field. The seams of coal are more numerous and their thickness greater than in any other portion of this coal field; it can be mined cheaper and with more economy generally, under the same rates of labor, than in any other in this country, without exception. The markets of the West, or the great Ohio and Mississippi Valleys, are open beyond any controlling competition to the trade of the Kanawha in coal, oil, salt, iron and lumber. Charleston is 200 miles nearer Cincinnati than Pittsburg, and always open to navigation; while the Ohio to Pittsburg is frequently closed by ice in the winter, and interrupted by low water in the summer. The principal volume of the great and rapidly increasing trade of the West may be diverted to the seaports of the East, *via* the Kanawha Valley, with much economy in time and transporting power.

We do not make these remarks as invidious comparisons. Nothing we can say will detract from Pittsburg; nor do we wish to say one word against that noble city and her vast resources. We only wish we could say to the helpless, dilatory Virginians, "Go ye and do likwise;" and we would willingly show them the way.

The geological reports on the coals of West Virginia make the number of workable seams to be 13; but 14 have been developed on the dividing ridge between the waters of the Great Kanawha and Coal Rivers, on a line with Lenn's Creek, and in all probability these are all below the Pittsburg seam. But here every seam appears to have reached a maximum size for the bituminous formations. While B and E are not as large as found in a few other localities, the intervening seams, which in other portions of the field are of no commercial or workable value, are here found in workable size, or from 2 to 3 feet in diameter. The number of workable seams are greater than those found within the same measures in Pennsylvania any place, not excepting the anthracite fields, though the total amount of coal is less than that which is found at many points in the anthracite regions. But were we to count all the seams, both small and large, in the western part of the anthracite measures, they would correspond nearly with the coal-seams found on the Great Kanawha. We have stated our belief, however, that the cannel coal-seams have no counterpart in the anthracite regions —that they appear within the rich bituminous shale, which does not exist in the Eastern measures; and consequently, three of the numerous seams in the Kanawha sections are thus accounted for.

We may also here notice a fact which may be interesting, and which may have some connection with the divisions of the seams in this locality, or *vice versa*.

It will be found farther on that the coal measures in Western Kentucky, and in the same geological range or position in the great basin with the Kanawha, are in like manner divided and represented by numerous small seams instead of a few large ones, as in some portions of the anthracite regions, where the coal measures reach the same elevation.

The seams which we give in the following table exist, we have reason to believe, under the Pittsburg seam, and do not, therefore, represent all the productive coal measures of West Virginia. There are still several seams found in the higher grounds back from the river, or on the head-waters of Elk, Coal, Gauley, and other large streams emptying into the Great Kanawha, Guyandotte, Big Sandy, &c. Yet we have not found the same productive condition in any other part of the Great Alleghany coal-field as compared with the measures between Coal and Kanawha rivers. The thickness of the strata is estimated in this table, but the seams have been practically developed.

A short distance above the conglomerate a small seam exists, not considered workable. But about fifty feet from the conglomerate a variable seam is found, ranging from five to ten feet in thickness: this coal in all probability lies below the level of Lenn's Creek, at the forks and is not found above *water-level.* Above this exists the large seam of iron ore to be noticed farther on. The third seam of coal appears to be small, but varies from two to four feet. The fourth is a cannel coal of about four feet, but varies from three to six feet. The fifth seam is a hard bituminous, ranging from two to four feet in thickness. The sixth is likewise bituminous, but not generally over three or four feet thick, and is sometimes smaller. The seventh seam, sometimes cannal coal, ranges from three to five feet thick. The eighth and ninth are hard, bituminous seams, from thirty inches to four feet thick. The tenth seam is generally large. ranging from seven to ten feet, but is divided by fire-clay, which sometimes, in practical effect, makes two workable seams of the one. The eleventh is a fine cannel seam, known as the "Peytona" (?) cannel, five to six feet thick. The twelfth, thirteenth aud fourteenth are not opened or developed, but, from appearances, are known to be seams of good workable dimensions, and one of them is supposed to be cannel. The average dimensions of the seams and the thickness of the intervening strata are about as given in the accompanying table:

DIMENSIONS OF SEAMS AND THICKNESS OF STRATA ON THE LAND BETWEEN KANAWHA AND COAL RIVERS.*

			Feet.	Feet.	
A	No.	1, coal on the conglomerate..............	30	2	A
B	"	2, coal and intervening measures....	50	6	B
	"	3, coal and " "	100	3	
	"	4, coal cannel " "	90	5	
C	"	5, coal " "	95	3	C
	"	6, coal " "	80	2½	
	"	7, coal sometimes cannel "	100	3	
D	"	8, coal " " "	85	2	D
E	"	9, coal " " "	90	2½	E
	"	10, coal " " "	50	10	
	"	11, coal cannel " "	100	6	
F	"	12, coal " "	100	4	F
?	"	13, coal cannel? " "	195	5?	
	"	14, coal " "	80	3?	
		Coal measures................................	1350 coal	50	

* The thickness of the measures is perhaps exagerated, as they are only estimates. The coal-seams, however, are actual developments as far as No. 11.

Perhaps nowhere in the State is the wealth of coal so conspicuously exposed as in the banks and bluffs of Elk river. This stream, whose banks are not over 10 or 15 feet high, in the neighborhood of Sutton, Braxton county, 90 miles from its mouth, actually gets down from 300 to 350 feet below the general level of the country, near the Clay county line, where its banks, steep, but densely covered with timber, appear like hills rising directly out of its bed. As a consequence, the shorter tributaries, having but a few miles in which to accomplish this heavy descending grade, are extremely rapid, and in furrowing and deepening their precipitous beds, are continually piling a large amount of detritues into the bed of Elk river, where the heaviest material, principally iron ore, forms the great bulk of the numerous shoals found in this vicinity. Not only in these ravines, but in the very face of the banks on the main stream, are the coal seams laid bare for miles in extent. Below the mouth of Birch, on Duck, Tate and O'Brien's creek, the largest of two or three workable seams is one of superior spint coal of 8 feet, and from 80 to 90 feet above the water level. Cannel coal is near at hand also, sometimes lining the bituminous coal veins or splitting them in two, then almost suddenly giving out to reappear farther down in the same eccentric forms. Near Clay Court House, and for 15 miles below, are seen veins of 5, 6, 8 and 9 feet of superior coal, some of it famous for its yield in distilled oil, which is fluid and stands at 27° Beaume, at a temperature of 60°. A large cannel coal vein is open at Queen's shoal below Clay Court House. On Falling Rock and on Mill creeks; large oil distilleries were in successful operation before the discovery of Petroleum, but are vacant now. The Falling Creek works were purchased since then by an Eastern company, who expects to resume developments at an early day.

The valleys of Coal river, Little Coal river, Mud river, Guyandotte and tributaries present but a repetition of the coal seams of Elk and Great Kanawha. Of this section the intelligent report of Thos. L. Broun, Esq., President of the Navigation Company of Coal river, for 1866 says:

"For quantity, quality, and variety of splint, cannel and bituminous coal, the Coal river region has been most favorably known since the year 1858, when the attention of capatalists in New York and elsewhere was first drawn to the remarkably rich deposits of cannel coal on this river by Col. Wm. M. Peyton, the pioneer spirit of the Coal river enterprise. From the forks of Coal river to Marsh and Clear Forks of Big Coal river,

a distance of forty miles, are found cannel coal, splint and bituminous coal in great abundance and of the very best quality. So likewise, are to be found similar deposits from the forks of Coal to Boone, C. H., on Little Coal, a distance of twenty miles. These veins vary from 2½ to 12 feet in thickness, and as many as five distinct, workable veins are found on the same property, lying horizontally and above the beds of the streams. At Peytona, in addition to veins of splint and bituminous coal, there are two distinct and workable veins of pure cannel coal, respectively 2½ to 3½ feet thick, the former lying about sixty feet above the other."

Not less than four Eastern companies, besides the pioneer "Peytona" are owning from 1500 to 5000 acres each, of coal and cannel coal lands on Coal river and branches, and are preparing for extensive developments. One of them lately made an experimental shipment of 12,000 bushels of cannel coal to *New York* via Parkersburg and the Baltimore & Ohio R. R.

Cannel coal brings at Cincinnati from 33 to 40 per cent. more than any other coal.

Alluding to the Pittsburgh coal trade Mr. Broun states, that in 1864 there were mined, in that vicinity, 48,462,966 bushels of coal, of which 29,541,597 were shipped down the Ohio river, swelled probably to 40,000,000 bushels by shipments from Pomeroy, Ohio, Wheeling, Mason City, and other points of the Ohio river, all of which had to pass by the mouth of the Kanawha river on its way to market, and might be supplied by the coal-fields of Kanawha, Elk and Coal rivers, at less cost, and owing to the freedom of these waters from ice, with less risk and greater regularity. Point Pleasant, at the mouth of the Great Kanawha, is 250 miles nearer Cincinnati than Pittsburgh, which gives the Kanawha coal an advantage of at least one cent per bushel on the cost of transportation. Obstruction by ice also constitutes an important element of risk in the shipment of Pittsburgh coal.

Another enormous difference in favor of this region exists in the respective price of land as stated by Mr. Broun. Coal lands on the Youghiogheny rate at $250 per acre; Monongahela $300 per acre, Alleghany $400 per acre, near Pennsylvania Central Railroad $450 near the city of Pittsburg $800 per acre, whilst far better coal lands on Kanawha, Elk and Coal rivers may be purchased at from $5 to $100 per acre, according to accessibility.

"In Hampshire county," says Prof. Rogers, "upon a stratum of valuable, iron, and not less than 15 feet in thickness, there rests a bed of sandstone upon which reposes a coal seam three feet thick, above this another bed of sandstone, then a two foot vein of coal, then sandstone, then another coal seam of 4 feet; again a stratum of sandstone, and over it a 7 foot vein of coal over this a heavy bed of iron ore; and crowning the series an enormous coal seam of from 15 to 20 feet in thickness."

Here is then an aggregate thickness of 35 feet of coal, with nearly 25 of iron are all accessible in the face of the same mountain. Fifteen thousand acres of land, supposed to contain nineteen feet of this coal, and situated in the new counties of Mineral and Grant, (taken from Hampshire and Hardy) were lately sold to Baltimore parties for the sum of $225,000. A similar sum was paid for 600 acres, including the Despard mines near Clarksburg, a 9 foot vein of superior gas coal, when gold ranged at $2.60.

The Clarksburg and Fairmont coals, whose reputation as gas coals is nowhere surpassed, are being extensively mined and shipped to Baltimore, New York and Philadelphia. Prof. Rogers regards this deposit, identical in both places, as one of the richest in the State. One of the seams, the main coal of Mr. Taylor, measures from 10 to 12 feet in thickness, below which, and separated chiefly by a heavy bed of sandstone there lies a thinner stratum of a more highly bituminous character. These valuable seams and others of the same group, which may be traced to Clarksburg all way up from Big Sandy river, through the counties of Wayne, Cabell, Boone, Lincoln, Kanawha, Clay, Braxton and Lewis, may be followed from Harrison county through Marion and Monongahela and the whole length of the Monongahela valley to Pittsburg.

Preston county also contains several available seams of coal, known as the 3, 4, 6, 8 and even 10 feet veins, the largest of which are being developed at Tunnelton, Newburg and at, or near Independence. Some of this mineral is said to be equal to Clarksburg coal for gas, and to yield ten thousand cubic feet of it, per ton. The same seams are said to extend through the counties of Barbour and Upshur, but whether they be identical or not, it is certain that both of these counties possess excellent bituminous coal, and possibly cannel coal also, which has been discovered at several points in the county of Preston.

In addition to the main seams of the Monongahela valley, Lewis county has not less than three or four seams from 2 to 5 feet thick of bituminous coal. Cannel coal and bituminous shale are also found near the western edge of this county, extending from the waters of Fink and Alum forks of Leading creek, southward to the Sandfork of Little Kanawha river, in Gilmer county. This latter county also contains at least one 6 foot seam of highly bituminous coal, and one of cannel on the Little Kanawha and tributaries, below Glenville, and though not yet minutely explored, the coal field of this region, accessible by water from Parkersburg, appears capable of an extensive supply.

The Western limit of the middle and upper group, containing the largest and richest seams, appears to dedescribe a curve or irregular semicircle, leaving the Ohio river below Moundsville, excluding the counties of Wetzel, Tyler, Doddridge, Ritchie, Pleasants, Wirt, Wood, Jackson, Calhoun & Roane, and returning to the Ohio river near the upper edge of Mason county, where the large seam of Pomeroy coal first makes its appearance. In the territory embraced between this curve and the Ohio river only the smaller seams have so far been discovered, varying from 4 to 2½ feet in thickness and even tapering down, in Wood county to 18 inches. In Doddridge county are found, at different levels, a 3 to 4 feet vein of excellent bituminous coal, and a bed of shales of the same thickness, both rich in fossils of tropical vegetation. On the Laurel fork of Goose Creek, White Oak oil region, Ritchie county, a superior seam of coal 4 feet thick is being developed for the Parkersburg market. In the same county, on McFarland's run, a small tributary of Hughes' river, 14 miles south of Cairo station, is found a vein of Asphaltum, or solidified Petroleum, which, from its geological position and probable origin constitutes one of the wonders of the continent. From the right hand fork of McFarland's run, in a direction N. 75° west towards the oil break, but two miles distant by an air line, the solid sandrock, which forms the main substance of surrounding strata appears to have been rent vertically by some unaccountable force below, to within a few feet of the top of the hills, and into the perpendicular fissure so created, from 4 to 5 feet wide, the mineral was injected, from unmistakable indications, in the liquid state. There are numerous theories afloat as to the probable connection of this wonderful lode with the oil belt in the same vicinity, and it is not unlikely that if the Asphaltum vein can be followed in its westward course below the water level, where it is supposed to dip a mile and a half, or more from its eastern end, some interesting discoveries will be made as to the nature and origin of both the oil belt and the Asphaltum.

This mineral, which is now being developed by a Company of Baltimore and New York capitalists, resembles ordinary bituminous coal in color and brilliancy, but very unlike coal, crumbles very readily into small fragments when handled. The company owning the deposit on McFarland's run, have erected well appointed chemical works, and constructed a wooden railroad to Cairo station. The Asphaltum produces upwards of one hundred and fifty gallons per ton of superior oil, 30° gravity, and has been experimented with for various other purposes, upon which the proprietors have not yet deemed expedient to enlighten the public. Untold wealth is expected to be realized from this remarkeable deposit, and surrounding lands, in which the presence of mineral is barely conjectured, are held at from $500 to $600 per acre.

Exact statistics in regard to the production and exportation of West Virginia coal are not easily obtained, but the following figures procured from the most reliable sources come sufficiently near the truth for practical purposes.

The mines of Great Kanawha, Coal, and Elk rivers, are reported to have shipped in 1869, upward of 4,500,000 bushels, or 162,000 tons. Clarksburg, Fairmont, Newburg and Tunnelton, principally gas coal, 360,000 tons. Mason City mines, opposite Pomeroy, 2,500 tons. Mineral county, or Piedmont mines 150,000 tons. Wheeling and a few minor points 30,000 tons. In round numbers a total of 600,000 tons, which at the average home value of $3 per ton, give a value of $1,800,000 as the total coal production of 1869.

In each one of the above mentioned localities preparations are making for increased development. At several points the production has quadrupled within the last three years.

Reducing the capacity of the 15,000 square miles of coal in the State to a single workable vein of 3 feet, we obtain an aggregate of 47,000,000,000 tons, to which the last annual production is as five-eigths of a ton, or a cart load to the acre. At this rate the supply would endure 78,400 years and if the development is increased twenty times, 3920 years.

The annual production of England is 95,000,000 tons, or more than one hundred and fifty times that of West Virginia, whose coal area exceeds that of England by 9000 miles, and that of the rest of Europe together 6000 miles.

COAL OIL.

The manufacture of coal oil from the rich cannel coal of the Kanawha, was extensively carried on in that region before the war, and practical men who know the cost and have calculated the profits by experience, state that, as a general rule, more money may be made in manufacturing this oil from the coal than by boring for it and obtaining it in a natural state. The one is certain and continuous, while the other is uncertain and precarious. The first depends upon skill and capital; the second on a fortunate "strike,"—which, unfortunately, is not the rule, but the exception: far more blanks than prizes are drawn from oil-wells.

But when the manufacturing of oil from coal is conducted with the proper skill and judgment, the results are certain. And in no place can this be done with more success than in the

Great Kanawha Valley, because in no other locality are there richer coals or a more abundant supply, while timber for barrels and other accessory means are abundant and available.

The best cannel coal, when properly treated on the large scale, yields 60 gallons of crude oil to the ton; and the cost of the mining and manipulation ought not to exceed $2.50 per ton,—which at even 10 cents per gallon in the tanks, would leave a large profit on the oil produced.

There is great improvement to be made in the manufacture of coal oil from the coal, and the cost of producing it may be reduced nearly one-half from the present estimates, which is from 25 to 30 cents per gallon for refinéd oil. We have noticed, particularly, several large items of expense in the production of the crude article which may be abated, but which in this connection we shall not discuss: it belongs properly to the department of Petroleum.

It will thus appear that the Great Kanawha Valley is not only a great natural mining and manufacturing region, but one that may enjoy the greatest trade that ever flowed from the mountains or the inland plains and valleys to the sea. The coal, iron, oil, and salt of this region are inexhaustible, and may be produced with the minimum of labor and expense, and consequently, the maximum of profits.

We have long beheld the vast mineral resources of this part of the Great Alleghany coal-field with professional admiration, and have frequently called attention to their value. If we now *seem* partial to West Virginia, we can prove that our affections have always turned towards her unlimited stores of coal and iron with an ardent desire to be able to pronounce the "open sesame" which should expose her treasures to the world.

[*Daddow's* "*Coal, Iron and Oil.*"

SALT.

The oldest and most productive salt manufacturing region in the State is known as the Kanawha Salines, and extends from a short distance above Charleston, twelve or fifteen miles on both sides of the Great Kanawha river, through one of the most interesting landscapes in the State, embracing the villages of Malden and Brownstown. There is plausible evidence that the Indians were acquainted with the Kanawha brine, and used some crude process for its evaporation. But it is only sixty years since the first salt well was bored here by white settlers. Since then the manufacturing of salt has become a leading feature in the Kanawha Valley, and laid the foundation to much of its prosperity and reputation.

Salt wells are sunk here in a manner very similar to

artesian and petroleum wells. Wooden casing is driven through the alluvial soil to the solid rock, through which the well is drilled, and cased with iron or copper tubes into the brine, which is reached at a depth of 800 to 1000 feet, or more. Then, drilling and tubing is continued, until a gas vent is struck below, which, rushing upward with wonderful power, not only forces the brine into the pans with a continuous flow, but under mechanical control, is made to serve the purpose of fuel in the evaporation. This economical feature is not found to any extent in any other saltworks on the continent, and materially reduces the cost of manufacturing in this locality. Before the discovery of the gas, the brine was pumped up by horse or steam power, and evaporated with coal from the adjoining hills. It then required about 20 or 25 horse power to pump two wells, and from 1 to 1¼ bushels of coal, of 80 pounds, to evaporate one bushel, or 50 pounds of salt, from 90 or 100 gallons of brine.

The Kanawha salt has long enjoyed a wide and merited reputation, and is regarded as unsurpassed for curing meat for exportation. It is now being manufactured of three grades, marked: Common, Fine, and Dairy; specimens of the latter, furnished by General Lewis Ruffner, were exhibited with other products of the State, at the Paris Universal Exposition and attracted favorable notice.

There are at present nine furnaces in active operation in the Kanawha Valley, representing a capital of $500,000, including land, and producing 160,000 bushels per month, worth at the rate of 50 cents per bushel, $960,000 per annum.

The development of this importaut resource has been more or less impeded in times past, by the want of local capital, and system in bringing it to market, as well as by the casualities of the late war, which bore heavily upon the Kanawha Valley. Within the last two years the salt business has resumed an upward tendency, and proper steps are being taken for its immediate extension. Some of the most eligible salt property in the valley, with buildings and fixtures, is awaiting capital for development, and offered for sale upon inviting terms.

By virtue of a consolidation of the Kanawha furnaces with the Ohio River Salt Company, which also includes the furnaces of Mason City, West Virginia, and Pomeroy, Ohio, and vicinity, the product of each furnace or section is turned into common stock, and draws a pro rata dividend on sales.

The salt wells of Mason county are not less rich in brine than those of the Kanawha, and fast increasing in number. There are at present thirteen furnaces in operation, of less aggregate capacity than those of the Kanawha, and whose production is reported now at near 500,000 bushels per annum.

Manufacturing salt with profit does not necessarily require a large capital, when brine and coal or gas are abundant, and the locality is convenient to shipment. For years before the war, salt manufacturing was carried on in a cheap way at Bulltown, Braxton county, and at Addison, the county seat of Webster, and but for the insufficiency of roads to market, would have assumed extensive proportions, the question of profit not being a subject of doubt.

The salt bearing sandstone formation, which, by a supposed deflection from its general level, comes nearer the surface at the Kanawha Salines, than in other sections of the valley, has been traced for a considerable distance up the river, toward the mountains, though experiments in boring, so far, met with no encouraging success. But if upon a certain quite plausible, geological theory, *large* deeply seated *gas vents* are an indication of salt, rather than of oil, then the basins of both Kanawha's bid fair to rival the most productive salt regions now known. In nearly all the valleys of these basins, so far investigated, gas bubbles and springs may be seen coming up through the very bed of the streams, and along the alluvial banks when overflowed, those which find vent on dry or high ground, and are probably much more numerous, escaping observation. The most remarkable phemomenon in this line is observable on Elk river, at the so-called "End of the World" bend, half a mile below the mouth of O'Bryans Creek, in Clay county, where a cluster of gas springs, of nearly one-eighth of an acre in extent, is boiling up through the bed of the river, near its northern bank. At a low stage of water these springs are easily ignited with a match, the flame flashing rapidly from bubble to bubble across the whole cluster. A similar gas vent, almost equal in extent, boils up through the river at Duffield's bend. Strong gas vents and burning springs are found in the Elk river valley, on Duck creek, Rock Camp, Lower Rock Camp, Little Otter runs, and at various points above Sutton, in Braxton county.

On Little Otter, a well, bored for oil upon the indications of gas springs, is now being developed for salt by New York parties. The Burning Springs on Steer Creek have long been noted landmarks, and strong gas springs are seen on Grass run and several points on the Little Kanawha, outside of the Oil Belt.

Sulphurous, brackish springs, called deerlicks, abound throughout the State, many of which are so strongly impregnated, that salt is frequently seen in the chrystalline state upon the surface of the spring, when evaporated in midsummer.

An interesting paragraph in regard to the cost and profits of salt manufacturing appears in Special Commissioner Well's Report, under the head of Salt, Coal and Lumber:

"3d. As regards the profits which result from the manufacture of salt in the United States under the present system, the Commissioner, in addition to the evidence previously presented will ask attention only to the following table, showing the cost of making salt at one of the principle furnaces on the Ohio River for the year 1868:

Number of bushels (of 56 pounds each) produced		327,000
Cost of barrels	$23,468 99 or	7.18 cents per bushel.
Cost of coal	19,902 19 or	6.09 " "
Wages and salaries	21,075 96 or	6.45 " "
Repairs and incidentals	10,584 50 or	3.24 " "
Total	75,031 64 —	22.95 " "

To this must be added the cost of transportation, interest, commissions, &c.

The cost of manufacturing 319,000 bushels of salt at the same furnace in 1860 was 12.38 gold per bushel, or (with gold at 133) 17.84 cents currency. The average market price of salt in 1869 was from 20 to 23 cents per bushel gold, or (with gold at 133) 26⅛ to 30⅝ cents currency. The price of salt in Cincinnati in 1868 was 48 cents currency. It thus appears that while the cost of manufacturing has advanced 5 cents per bushel, currency, since 1868. Salt advanced 17 to 22 cents per bushel. The Commissioner could name the rate of dividend paid during the year 1868 by the furnacs referred to, were it not communicated confidentially. The reader can, however, approximately determine it by calculation."

The Commissioner also cites the following communication, addressed to him by the agent of one of the largest salt producing associations in West Virginia:

"The cost of making salt here is very variable, and dependent not only in a large degree upon the quality of the brine and size of furnace, but upon the personal energy of the proprietor and his acquaintance with the business. There are some of our furnaces which are operated with very slight or no profit, while others, by the purchase of superior property, and free investment of capital and skill, are enabled to make substantial profit. A furnace with a capacity of less than two hundred thousand bushels per annum is not a profitable investment here —I mean will not invite investment, although such furnaces are operated here, because the small profit will keep the property in repair, which one year's inactivity will almost destroy. A furnace having that capacity, if it can be increased to say two hundred and fifty thousand bushels, *will find the extra quantity almost entire profit.* A larger increase in quantity would require much more capital, but still the proportionate profit is greater on all above two hundred thousand bushels."

IRON.

The mineral of industrial value next abundant in West Virginia, is iron, which is almost co-extensive with coal, though not present in seams quite as thick or as numerous. Iron ore is so generally prevalent in various forms throughout the State, that it would probably be more difficult to surmise where it is not, than where it may be found.

The great magnetic iron ore beds of North Carolina and Southern Virginia are not supposed to extend far into West Virginia, but immediately west of Alleghanies the scarcely less valuable beds of hematite, oxides and peroxides of iron merge into the great coal region of New river, and the Kanawha valley, extending west to the Ohio river, south across Coal, Guyandotte and Big Sandy rivers to the Kentucky line, and north up the valleys of Gauley, Elk and Pocatalico rivers.

Almost throughout the whole of this favored region, iron ore alternates in the same hills with coal, free from sulphur, with lime necessary to flux it, and with the fire clay, hydraulic lime and sandstone required in the construction of furnaces, while on the surface flourishes a bountiful supply of timber convertible into charcoal for the manufacture of steel. Yet in the whole of this mineral field, there is not to be found a single furnace to elevate this important ore above the rank and value of common clay.

From the Coal river region across Great Kanawha and up Elk river, iron ore is scarcely out of reach for a hundred miles. It occurs here in broken and continuous beds, principally as carbonates and oxides yielding from 50 to 80 per cent. of pure metal. Similar results are obtained from analysis of iron ores from Nicholas county. A very interesting mineral survey of the Elk river region was made years ago by M. Duplessis, a French engineer, who collected and analyzed many valuable specimens. Unfortunately his notes are not now accessible.

Following down the Little Kanawha valley, ferruginous shales and other indications of iron are prominent features of the country. Good specimens have been picked up on tributaries in the counties of Braxton, Gilmer, Calhoun and Wirt. Nodular or kidney iron ore is found in small beds, and in close proximity to coal and lime, as far north and east as the headwaters of Hughes' river and Leading creek.

Large and valuable seams are known in the counties of Randolph, Upshur and Barbour. In the latter county a furnace was worked several years ago. Lewis, Harrison and Taylor counties claim large deposits of superior ore, in close conjunction with limestone and coal; but the iron beds of Monongalia and Preston seem to have attracted earlier attention. On Cheat river eight miles east of Morgantown, the Jackson furnaces were in operation years ago, but stopped since for the want of cheap access to the ore, several miles away. In Preston, near Independence station, the Franklin furnace is now in full blast, turning out 10 tons of pig iron per day, at a cost of $25 per ton. The average price in the Wheeling market, distant 115 miles by rail is $36 per ton.

In regard to abundance, quality and accessibilty of necessary materials, these works possess unusual advantages. Immediately above the water level of Three Forks river appears an 8 feet vein of superior bituminous coal, free from sulphur, and yielding excellent coke. Above an intervening conglomerate rock, appears a 2½ feet vein, and close above a 4 feet vein of coal. The next mineral seams, all separated by strata of sand rock, are, one of coal 4 feet, an 18 inch iron vein, and a little higher up, a 3 feet vein of superior ore, then 3 feet of limestone, and near the top of a hill a 12 inch vein of ore. These veins are all workable, but reducing the average thickness to 2 feet, the capacity of one acre of land here is equal to 5000 tons of ore.

The ore of this vicinity and of Laurel Hill, and across the mountains to the Upper Potomac is regarded as among the best in the State, and yields from 60 to 80 per cent of pure metal.

A gray ore, reported to contain from 45 to 60 per cent. pure iron, is found near a fossiliferous bed of clay shales, fire clay, and limestone, at Washington's Bottom, 10 miles below Parkersburg, and is supposed to extend inland for several miles. Half way between this bed and the mouth of Little Kanawha there is being opened a vein of hematite, fossil ore, from 10 to 12 feet in thickness, supposed to extend through four or five thousand acres, reaching within a mile of the city of Parkersburg. Analysis shows this ore to contain from 45 to 50 per cent. of pure iron, and over 15 per cent. of lime. Timber being quite abundant in the vicinity, a charcoal furnace is suggested as the cheapest mode of development. Strong indications of iron exist in other parts of Wood and Pleasants counties, but have not been much investigated. Good specimens of nodular iron ore are shown in Ritchie county, and a bed of this ore from 8 to 10 feet thick is found on Arnold's creek, 4 miles below Central station, in Doddridge county. Similar deposits are supposed to exist in Tyler, Wetzel and Marion and the Panhandle counties, and are being continually reported from different localities in the State, where, owing to the depth of overlying earth on the hillsides, only faint indications could be observed heretofore. There is no question, but that not one half of the iron beds in the State have not yet been brought to light, and that scientific exploration will greatly enlarge the field of discovery.

PETROLEUM.

When the heat and smoke of the memorable oil excitement of 1864 and 1865 subsided, the few surviving, profitable developments were found to range nearly in a straight line, within a strip of country from one to two miles wide, extending from the Little Kanawha river, at Burning Spring run, North 10° East, through the counties of Wirt, Ritchie, Wood and Pleasants, and crossing Hughes river a few miles above its forks, the Baltimore and Ohio R. R. at Petroleum station, the N. W. Turnpike at Sand Hill, and the Ohio river near the mouth of French creek, West Virginia, two miles below the town of St. Mary's, and embracing the localities since become famous, under the names of Oil Rock, Standing Stone, California, Laurel Fork, Oil Spring Run, Gales Fork, White Oak, Horseneck and Rawson's Run.

Although millions had been invested in oil lands and boring operations all over the State, *not a single paying well was struck, then or since, outside of this Belt.* This result had been predicted and warned against as early as 1861, by Prof. E. B. Andrews of Marietta, who took conscientious pains to expound the theory of the Oil Belt or "Break" upon scientific principles. Unfortunately one class of "oil men" cared nothing for science, and the truth did not subserve the purposes of the other.

The Oil Belt of West Virginia, also termed the great

upheaval, or uplift, essentially differs in its geological structure from the country on either side of it. Here the usual horizontal stratification is suddenly interrupted by a disturbance, as if a gigantic mole, with its back a mile broad, had burrowed its way several hundred feet under the surface, and forced the overlying strata to the right and left into an anticlininical, roof-shaped bulge, or fold. Geologists still differ as to the true cause of this phenomenon. Some attribnte it to the same plutonic action that elevated the Alleghanies, and assume that several such belts and breaks may exist above or below the surface, steadily rising from the Ohio valley to the mountains; and as a proof, cite the synclinical out crop of the upheaved West Virginia strata in reverse order, and in nearly parallel direction, in Athens, Washington and Noble counties, Ohio. Others regard the belt as the effect of powerful lateral pressure, caused by shrinkage in the course of the drying of the earth's crust, when still in a semi-plastic state, during one of the *dry* intervals of sedimentary deposit.

This break, with its anti-clinical edges, is distinctly traced from the Little Muskingum oil regions in Ohio, to the Little Kanawha river at Burning Spring Run, West Virginia. Here it seemingly dips into, and disappears in the higher hills south of the river without exhibiting any farther sign of disturbance, *on the surface*, until its underground course reaches the Burning Spring in the Great Kanawha valley. Only here, where instead of petroleum, rise those powerful gas vents alluded to in the chapter on salt, a slight dip or undulation is perceptible in the stratification. In the drawing of the "Oil Belt" given in the appended map, the section *a b* illustrates the break as it now appears at Burning Springs, *f f* the horizontal strata deposited after the uplift and before erosion, and *a a* the aspect of the break on the railroad, between Eaton's and Petroleum station. In the latter section the horizontal deposits, accumulated after the disturbance, have been entirely abraded and washed away, and even the apex of the fold, still visible at Burning Springs at *e*, is entirely gone, leaving a mile and a half between the steepest uplifted strata east and west. This gap is filled by a sedimentary mass, evidently lifted up from below, slightly bent and deflected by the force of the operation, and to the great surprise of some geologists, containing, a few yards above the water level, a 4 feet vein of highly bituminous coal.

Farther investigations may finally decide the still disputed question as to the cause of disturbance, or break, and the nature and origin of petroleum itself. In the meantime at least two points, essential for practical purposes, are settled beyond a doubt: 1st, that no matter what subterranean conditions, favorable to the generation or accumulation of oil, may exist outside of this belt, there are no reliable surface indications of the same, to guide the location of wells. 2d, That petroleum, though perhaps percolating through the lime and sand rocks of the entire State at proper depths and levels, can only be found in paying quantities, *where fissures, caves and crevices favor its accumulation and retention.*

The most productive wells were struck since at different points of the belt, on the inner edge of the anticlinicals at *d* (see map) where the unconformable joints between the vertical and the horizontal strata, leave the greatest opportunity for a vacuum. Boring wells upon any other indications in West Virginia, must ever be more or less of a lottery, until something more is known of the underground structure of the country. Every where outside of the break, burning springs, and gas springs, and even petroleum springs, only served to delude the operator.

After 1865, oil developments in West Virginia rapidly assumed a more legitimate character and extensive proportions, in the hands of skillful and enterprising parties, many of whom had acquired experience in the oil regions of Pennsylvania. The region first developed extended from Burning Spring Run to California, near the forks of Hughes river, and from Rawson's run and Horseneck to the Ohio river, the main center of operations remaining on the Rathbone Tract, and vicinity, where the most famous wells, such as the Karnes and Camden, Rathbone, Eternal Center, Shattuck, Waite and Otterson, were successively struck. Some of these, bored to a depth of 400 to 600 feet, flowed for many weeks from 250 to 500 barrels per day, then subsided to 100, and then to 50, until reduced to 5 or 6 barrels under the pump. Within the last three years, old, exhausted wells were deepened to 1000 or 1200 feet, with highly satisfactory results.

The number of wells now worked in this section is reported at twenty-seven, pumping respectively from 5 to 50 barrels per day, only one of them, the Newberger & Braidon well, claiming the latter figure. The aggregate production falls but little short of 300 barrels per day, or 80,000 barrels per annum, giving at the present rate of 15 cents per gallon, $480,000 for 300 working days. Prices have varied from 13 to 16¾ cents per gallon during the year 1869, which is regarded as encouraging to more extensive development. All of this oil finds a ready cash market, for purposes ef refining and exportation, at Parkersburg, distant from Burning Springs, by river, 38 miles.

The petroleum obtained here is a superior article of light, or illuminating oil, from 36 to 42° gravity, the heaviest grades coming from the deepest wells. The light oil obtained throughout the Belt varies somewhat in color, and several degrees in gravity.

The section of the Break embraced between the Baltimore & Ohio Railroad and the Northwestern Turnpike, in Wood and Ritchie connties, containing 6 or 7 square miles, and drained by the Laurel and Gales' Forks, and Oil Spring Run of Goose Creek, the White Oak and Mud Lick Fork of Walker's Creek, is known as the " Heavy Oil, or White Oak Region," and up to the summer of 1869, yielded exclusively a heavy article, from 32° to 28°, and on Gales Fork even 26° to 25½° gravity, from wells varying from 300 to 500 feet in depth. Several large flowing wells like the Longmoor, Harkness, Gale, Barber and Atwater, at one time attracted large investments to this section. Since then a number of them measurably exhausted, were bored several hundred feet deeper, and are now yielding a light oil, similar to that obtained in the residue of the Belt.

The heavy oil of this section is exclusively used in its crude state as a lubricator on railroad and other machinery, and simply purified from water and other extraneous matter, by settling in tank; and freed from grit by a process of heating or steaming, not injurious to the lubricating quality of the oil. The present production of pure lubricating oil does not exceed 25,000 barrels per annum, while the consumption, in the United States alone, is estimated at 300,000 barrels, the difference being supplied by adulterations and imitations. These are manufactured chiefly at Cincinnati, Cleveland, Pittsburgh, New York and Philadelphia, frequently under West Virginia trade marks. The principle ingredients used, are crude light oil, condensed by evaporation or partial distillation, paraffine, coal tar, and the residuum of refineries. The most reliable test of genuiness consists in the application of ice, under which the spurious article will congeal, while the genuine retains its fluidity.

As the present production of light and heavy oil in West Virginia does not exceed 110,000 barrels per annum, from a belt of forty square miles, recognized as genuine boring territory, development may be regarded as scarcely begun. At present, operators tenaciously cling around the productive centers, avoiding new and untried territory, which is also less favored with transportation facilities. Seven miles of pipe, including a few short branches, through which the oil is propelled by stationary engines, are now in operation from Sand Hill through Volcano station, on the White Oak fork, to Petroleum station, and an extension South of the railroad toward Burning Springs is in contemplation.

Laurel Junction, two miles west of Petroleum is reached from Volcano by a zigzag railroad four miles in length. The rate of freight by the pipe depends upon the length of route and competition. Freight per Volcano railroad to Laurel Junction, is 45 cts. per barrel of

40 or 45 gallons, thence to Parkersburg 40 cents, and to Baltimore $1.56 per barrel. To Baltimore, in tank cars, 3¾ cents per gallon.

Transportation from Burning Springs to Parkersburg, in bulk, costs 1 cent per gallon, in barrels per barges and flatboats, 50 cents per barrel. A large increase of developments in the Burning Springs region is expected upon the completion of the Little Kanawha improvement by locks and dams, promised for 1870, which will permit the shipping of oil to market at the most favorable stage of the market without regard to season.

The greater part of the lubricating oil produced, is tanked at Petroleum, Laurel Junction, and Parkersburg. The current supply at the latter point averages 10,000 barrels.

The price of genuine oil land, within the Belt, and surrounded by productive wells, varies from $2000 to $5000 per acre, but is now seldom paid, operators preferring to lease, by paying a bonus of $500 to $1000 per acre, and a royalty of ⅛ to ⅓ on the production. Undeveloped tracts, extending across the Break, and including land on one or both sides of it, may still be bought at from $25 to $100 per acre, and a royalty of from 1-8 to 1-5 in addition.

OTHER MINERALS.

Shortly after the collapse of the great oil excitement of 1864 and 1865, disappointed speculators made an attempt to transfer the excitement from petroleum to gold, silver and lead. This paroxism, however, was shortlived, and received its quietus, after sinking a few hundred thousand dollars more in useless holes and shafts, in various sections of the State.

Specimens of lead are still being mysteriously shown through the country, as having been obtained in out of the way places, which somehow, appear destined to remain nameless, but may possibly yet be divulged, there being no geological reason why this mineral should not exist in West Virginia. As for schemes of gold and silver in the coal measures of this State, they may be regarded as hopelessly exploded.

The existence of copper in West Virginia, though asserted from time to time upon slight indications, is not yet a fixed fact. Of Antimony, good specimens have been repeatedly shown, but never yet traced to the original deposit. Iron pyrites, or fools gold, which is often found in seams several inches thick, has contributed much to perpetuate popular delusions about precious metals.

On the other hand, the more unpretending, but intrinsically valuable limestone in all its modifications, is a familiar feature of the country. It always occurs in the proximity of coal, and quite abundantly without it. In the valleys of the Kanawha basin, a strongly hydraulic limestone abounds, frequently designated and used as cement. The Greenbrier, Monongahela and Tygarts valleys, and the table lands, exhibit miles of uninterrupted limestone soil. In the Potomac counties, limestone forms the principal constituent of the soil and yields from 60 to 90 per cent of pure lime. There also is found a friable marl much valued as a fertilizer, and capable of sustaining the grain crops of that fruitful section for centuries. A similar deposit somewhat more tenacious is exposed in the beds of many streams west of the mountains, where it is used by the pioneers as "whitewash."

The whole belt containing the main coal seam from Pennsylvania to the Kentucky line, is emphatically styled a limestone country, and again, nearly the whole of the Northwestern turnpike from Parkersburg to Winchester, was macadamized with hard limestone found within reach. Near Weston in the county of Lewis, there are quarries of a fine grained blue limestone, used in the foundation of the Hospital for the Insane, and susceptible of a beautiful finish.

The Panhandle counties also contain large seams of limestone, which are conspicuously exposed in the hills around Wheeling.

Analyses of bottom lands and of apparently strongly vegetable soils, in sections where no limestone is seen around for miles, show the presence of more or less lime for a considerable depth.

Fire clay, yellow, gray and white, is quite common in several counties, as well as Potter's clay of various qualities. Large banks of superior plastic clay are supplying extensive potteries at Parkersburg, Morgantown and other points. Similar beds are reported from nearly all the counties containing coal. In many localities, a seam of very fine white or blueish clay, highly plastic, usually lines the upper edge of the smaller coal and cannel coal seams. Two varieties of superior clay underlie the iron ore vein near Wasnington's Bottom, in Wood county. Large pebbles, or cobble stones, said to be reducible into superior fire clay, are found imbedded in the laminated sand rocks of the central counties.

The Sandstone, white, yellow and gray, is diffused in greater aggregate thickness and more compact masses than any other strata of the coal measures. About one half of it occurs in large solid seams, is fine grained and easily worked, and constitutes a handsome and durable building material. The other half is irregularly laminated, somewhat hard and shelly, and more micaceous. Grindstones may be manufactured in almost any section, and a valuable mill grit, or burrstone is developed in Laurel hill, and probably abounds at other points in the mountains. A very hard conglomerate stone, possibly the millstone grit mentioned by some geologists as overlying the petroleum rocks, crops out on a branch of Spring Creek, four miles south of Burning Spring Run, in Wirt county, and when polished, resembles variegated marble, and appears well adapted to architectural uses.

A large deposite of white sand, which supplies the glass factories at Wheeling, is developed in Marion county and forms a source of considerable profit.

Alum, and Sulphate of Iron, or Copperas, are often found in the chrystalline state on the outside of banks of sandrock and shales, where they were gradually deposited by small percolating springs. These substances are used in the country for various domestic purposes, principally for dyeing yarn and home made cloth.

MINERAL SPRINGS.

Of these natural attractions West Virginia may boast of a more liberal share than any other State, and yet it is fair to presume that much remains to be discovered under this head within her limits. The famous White Sulphur, in the county of Greenbrier, have long since established a reputation for the healing waters of our mountains, and leave nothing to desire in regard to scenery, buildings, tasteful grounds, and accommodation. From four to five thousand guests, from North and South, were registered there in the summer of 1869.

The mineral waters are furnished here by a single copious spring, of which the following analysis is given by Prof. Rogers, without proportions in figures: Sulphate of lime and of magnesia, clorides of sodium of calcium, and of magnesium, peroxide of iron, phosphate of lime, sulphate and hydrate of sodium, organic matter, sulphur and iodine. The gaseous matter consists of sulphurated hydrogen, carbonic acid, nitrogen and oxigen. The remedial virtues of this water extend chiefly to diseases of the liver, kidneys, alimentary canal, scrofula, rheumatism and neuralgia."

The White Sulphur Springs are now reached by rail from the East, and by river and turnpike from the West. Coaches leave Charleston, on the Kanawha, daily during the watering season.

The Blue Sulphur Spring in the same county is also beautifully located, and its waters, very similar in properties to the White Sulphur, gush forth at the rate of fifteen gallons per minute.

In the adjoining county of Monroe, not less than three mineral springs enjoy a wide spread popularity. These are the Red Sulphur, the Salt Sulphur, and the Sweet Sulphur, all of which are easily accessible from White Sulphur, and very similar in chemical composition and medical virtues. The Sweet Sulphur is reputed as particularly efficacious in female complaints.

All of these watering places are situated in a highly picturesque and interesting country.

The celebrated Berkeley Springs, the property of the State, are situated in Morgan county, two and a half miles from St. John's Run Station, on the Baltimore & Ohio Railroad. Their historic fame dates from the patronage of Gen. Washington, who with other great men of his time "attested their virtues, and built cottages there for summer residence." The waters though not highly impregnated with mineral ingredients, are of undoubted virtue, and for copiousness constitute a curiosity among such resorts on either side of the Atlantic. The supply of the bath rooms exceed twelve hundred gallons per minute, and the temperature of the fluid is 74° Fahr. In addition to this spring, there is a fountain of strongly stimulating chalybeate waters. The accommodations of this establishment are of a superior order, and are annually patronized by a refined and distinguished class of visitors.

The Capon Springs are situated in the adjoining county of Hampshire, on the west side of North mountain.

Five miles above Charlestown, in Jefferson county, near the banks of the Shenandoah river, are the Shanondale Springs, surrounded by one of the most captivating landscapes in the whole of this famous valley. This Spring is of a saline chalybeate character, and efficacious in all complaints requiring tonic remedies.

The Parkersburg Mineral Wells, situated 6 miles from the city of that name, and 2 miles from the Little Kanawha river, first attracted attention twenty years ago, and were liberally patronized until the beginning of the late war. This establishment is at present in want of a proprietor, or manager of some enterprise and capital. The accommodations, which need repairs, are ample for one hundred and fifty guests. The waters are supplied by four wells, of composition and virtue similar to the Monroe county springs, and slightly differing from each other in their mineral proportions. The site of the Wells is commanding, and the scenery, though of a more subdued character than that around the mountain springs, is not destitute of picturesque charm.

Strongly remedial sulphur springs have been used for some time near Martinsburg and Weston, and are found in several remote points in the State, where they attract little or no attention.

MANUFACTURING.

If from the chapters on wool-growing, timber and minerals, a glimpse may be obtained of the boundless manufacturing resources of West Virginia, the imagination will lose itself in conjectures, when in addition to the rest, her unfathomed wealth of water-power is taken into consideration.

The following remarks of the Commissioner of Statistics for Minnesota could not be more to the point, if written with special reference to our own State:

"Apart from social causes and the general influence of the stimulating and exacting climates of the North, in developing the forms of skilled industry, it is owing chiefly to two physical circumstances that New England has attained her present eminence in manufactures, in spite of her deficiency in the useful minerals and the raw material employed in the arts. These are, first, her abundant water power; and, second, her favorable commercial position which has enabled her to obtain ready supplies of raw material from abroad and to distribute the product through a wide range of dependent markets. These circumstances alone among the physical conditions of manufacturing power, have raised the little State of Massachusetts, without internal resources of raw material, without coal or iron, to the first rank among American States in the manufacture especially of textile fabrics. And these purely physical conditions of industrial development exist in our State in a greater degree than in New England, and in addition she possesses to a large extent essential elements of raw material of which New England is destitute."

From another source we learn that

"Ten thousand horse power at Lowell, Massachussetts, has collected a population of 40,000, and produces an annual value in manufactures of $24,000,000. Fall River has a population of 23,000, and a valuation of 17,000,000. Lawrence, with a power equal to Lowell's has already a population of 30,000. Biddford and Saco, with 3,500 horse power, have a population of 16,000;

4,200 horse in operation at Lewiston have already collected 22,-000 population and $8,000,000 valuation. In general a population of 1,000 may be looked for in each 166 horse-power employed in textile or equivalent manufactures."

Fifteen thousand sq. miles of West Virginia, or nearly twice the entire area of Massachusetts, are copiously watered by streams deriving hydraulic power from a fall of from five to ten feet per mile. In the absence of a hydrographical or topographical survey of the State, it is impossible to estimate with accuracy the amount of power at any given point. Nor is it at all necessary, because capitalists contemplating investment in this class of property will take ample pains for practical investigation, their greatest difficulty, here, being the embarrassment of choice. Their itinerary will begin at Harper's Ferry, where the famous water power, once belonging to the United States Armory, was lately purchased for over a quarter of a million dollars by a company of New England manufacturers, of which Gov. Sprague of Rhode Island is a member. Hence their path will lead them up the endless rapids of the Potomac river and branches, to the very foot of the Alleghany mountains. On the western slope they will descend the valleys of the Cheat, Tygart, Buckhannon, Monongahela, Little Kanawha, Elk, Greenbrier, Gauley, New, Great Kanawha, Guyandotte and Sandy river, as far west as a certain curved line of falls and rapids, mentioned in the chapter on timber, and distinctly traceable from the mouth of Cheat river below Morgantown, to the Falls of Big Sandy river, twelve miles above its forks. West of that line, the streams assume a more placid course, and ripples, affording good water-power, are less frequent. Yet there are many excellent manufacturing sites downward to within a few miles of the Ohio river, having, for the present at least, the advantage of proximity to transportatation, over many others in the mountains.

With the exception of grist and saw mills, carding machines and a few woolen mills, but few establishments in the State are now availing themselves of this water power, which, in sections remote from rail and navigable streams, does not even enhance the value of the surrounding lands. There, not a few landowners may be found, who will cheerfully donate the power with a spacious site adjoining, to induce settlement to the vicinity.

In regard to the actual products of manufactures in the State, reliable data are so scant, and so unequal in amount from different localities, that few figures can be given of practical value to the enquirer. The last Census furnishes little or nothing under this head, and the Auditor's report discloses nothing beyond the fact that the aggregate value of personal property listed by manufactures is $1,409,576, over one-half of which is credited to the city of Wheeling. From the fact that fourteen counties, including Kanawha, are omitted from this statement, it cannot well be consulted for practical purposes.

From an interesting pamphlet lately published by Dr. James E. Reeves, Health officer of the city of Wheeling, it appears that six iron and nail factories there, are employing, at present, 2295 workmen. Those six mills (including one at Bellaire, Ohio, opposite Benwood) produce 17,350 kegs of nails per week, or about 902,200 kegs per annum, at an average value of $4,-059,900. Besides these, and other rolling mills for the manufacture of railroad bar, rod, hammer iron, sheet iron, bridge iron, bolts, etc., there are two spike mills, which turn out annually, for railroad and boat building purposes, from 50,000 to 60,000 kegs. Another mill produces 60 tons of railroad bar per day, and last year furnished fifty miles of rails for the Pacific road. Hinge and tack factories are manufacturing very superior ware, and are rapidly extending their trade.

The foundries and machine shops employ 475 persons, and 60 more are occupied in the extensive machine shops of the Baltimore & Ohio Railroad Company. The foundries supply a very large trade in stoves and other castings, and have lately extended their production to iron fronts for houses, etc.

Six extensive glass works employ 860 persons of both sexes, and the amount of their products, some of which are of very superior style and finish, exceeds $600,000 per annum.

Two oil refineries produce upon an average 200 barrels of oil per week. Ten breweries manufacture upward of sixty thousand barrels of ale and lager beer. One distillery in operation returns 150 gallons of whiskey per day. The annual product of six tanneries is valued at $300,000.

In addition to the above, there are in flourishing activity carriage and wagon factories, cigar and tobacco factories, a woolen mill, merchant flouring, saw and planing mills and sash factories, marble works, a calico printing establishment, drug laboratories, furniture, copperware, harness and trunk factories, and other branches whose annual production is not reported.

First class steamboats are built and completely finished here, and furnished with the most improved machinery from Wheeling shops.

The city of Wheeling, from its earliest days, readily caught the spark of progress from the free soil breeze crossing the narrow Panhandle in either direction, and the solid nature and legitimate success of her enterprises gradually developed that high commercial character, liberality and public spirit, which commends her business men as examples to other communities in the State.

The salt production of Kanawha and Mason county is given in the mineral chapter. In addition to salt, Mason county manufactures 7000 kegs of nails per month, at the Clifton Works, which employ upward of 1300 hands.

The manufactured products of Parkersburg were carefully canvassed in 1865, and stated at an aggregate of $1,311,000, which has largely increased since, principally through the erection of additional oil refineries. There are at present seven of these establishments in operation here of a total capacity of 2500 barrels of refined oil per week, representing at the average price 30 cents per gallon, an annual production of over $1,700,000. The other manufacturing establishments consist of the large saw mills, planing mills, a sash, implement and wooden ware factory, one steam barrel factory of a capacity of 200 tight barrels per day, several large cooper shops, three foundries, two machine shops, besides the repair shop of the Balt. &Ohio R. R. Co., two tanyards, one pork packing establishment, several cigar and tobacco factories. two potteries, one steamboat yard, gas factory, &c. A rolling and nail mill has been in contemplation for sometime, and if not sooner erected, will certainly be called into existence whenever the improvement of the Kanawha river secures a cheap and regular supply of fuel.

Manufacturing estabishments similar to the above, exist to less extent at a number of other points in the State, such as Wellsburg, Fairmont, Clarksburg, Martinsburg, Piedmont and Charleston. Clarksburg has a first class foundry, machine shop and sawmill factory, and a woolen manufacturing company with a large capital has just been organized.

Tanneries, grist and sawmills, are found in every county, but carding machines are as yet not equal to neighborhood wants. Woolen factories producing cloth, jeans, linseys and flannels, are found in fifteen or twenty counties, and according to the last Census, over half a million dollars worth of these goods, including blankets, hosiery, carpets, &c., are annually produced in a domestic way, every operation, from the shearing of the wool to its final transformation by the loom, the carding alone excepted, being performed strictly in the "family circle."

It is scarcely necessary to add, that the above reference to manufactural productions exclusively of the city of Wheeling, was made, less to exhibit what was being done, than what is left to be accomplished by imported capital, skill and experience, in one of the wealthiest and most neglected industrial fields on the continent.

The condition and prospects of lumber manufacturing are given as accurately as possible under the head of "Timber". In the meantime West Virginia, in addition to nearly all of her dry goods, groceries, hardware, and fancy goods, *imports* steamboats, pine lumber and shingles, furniture, carriages, wagons, mowing machines, ploughs and other agricultural implements, wine and cider presses, churns, washtubs, pails and buckets, bread trays, washboards, wooden clocks, toys, rolling pins, sieves, brooms, and a number of smaller wooden articles "too tedious to mention."

INTERNAL IMPROVEMENTS.

The prospects of internal improvements have never been so bright as at present. Situated upon the direct route between the great western fields of production and the principal ports of the Atlantic, West Virginia can no longer be avoided by railway and water lines, *seeking the shortest connexions.* In the meantime, notwithstanding her long neglect under the tutelage of the mother State, she really possesses more turnpikes and river-improvements than local enterprise and statesmanship have, so far, been able to complete or to repair.

RAILROADS.

The Baltimore and Ohio Railroad, is the property of an independent corporation, and one of the most solid and best managed lines in America. It enters the State of West Virginia by the gates carved through the Blue Ridge by the Potomac at Harper's Ferry, and after traversing the eastern counties for a distance of 98 miles, crosses the river near Cumberland and follows the Maryland shore for 25 miles to New Creek station. Here, after reentering the State and passing the mining and manufacturing town of Piedmont, the State line is crossed again, and the ascent of the main Alleghany ridge is accomplished in 17 miles, on a grade of 116 feet to the mile. After traversing the Glades, and recrossing into West Virginia near Cranberry Summit, the road winds through the famous Cheat river and mountain scenery to Grafton, where it diverges northwest to Wheeling, and west to Parkersburg. At both of these points, bridges are under construction across the Ohio river, to connect the tracks with the Ohio Central and Marietta and Cincinnati railroads, both of which are under the control of the Baltimore and Ohio Company, and largely contribute to the trade and travel through West Virginia.

The distance from Baltimore to Wheeling by rail is 379 miles, from Baltimore to Parkersburg 383 miles, and the whole extent of the road through the State or along its line on the Potomac, 370 miles, including 15 miles of the Winchester branch from Harper's Ferry through the county of Jefferson.

The traffic of two-thirds of the State in point of surface, and of three-fourths in population, is at present more or less directly tributary to this road; which since its completion, fifteen years ago, has enhanced the value of real estate for many miles inland, from 100 to 300 per cent. Its western railway connections reach to the Pacific Ocean, while two lines of steamers respectively to Liverpool and Bremen, extend its traffic to the heart of Europe.

The natural and historical scenery along the route in Maryland and both Virginias, excites the wonder and admiration of the most experienced travelers. As a work of science and persevering skill, this road is one of the boldest triumphs over defiant and rugged nature. The tunneling on both branches amounts to over six miles, and for many miles more the track skirts and winds along precipices never before attempted in railroad engineering, and yet such is the perfection of the construction and management of the road that its merited reputation for safety and comfort is superior to that of any road of the same length on the most favorable ground.

Next in extent if not greater in importance to the State is the *Chesapeake and Ohio Railroad*, destined to connect one of the great Pacific railroads with the harbor of Norfolk, reputed deeper and more spacious than the port of New York, which now wields the sceptre of maritime commerce in the western hemisphere. This improvement once completed, the southern half of the State, by far the richest in mineral and manufacturing resources, will be thrown wide open to capital, enterprise and immigration, and the traditional croaking about West Virginia's neglected resources will cease forever.

The Chesapeake and Ohio Railroad, formerly known as the Virginia Central and Covington and Ohio Railroad, is now completed and in active operation from the Atlantic to White Sulphur Springs in West Virginia, a distance of 330 miles. From this point, the road is located and under construction down Greenbrier river, New river and Kanawha river to Coalsmouth, 10 miles below Charleston, where it leaves the valley for the hills, and after crossing Mud river and Guyandotte river, strikes the Ohio below the mouth of the latter stream, near the town of the same name. Thence a short run along the banks of the Ohio, brings it to the mouth of Big Sandy river, where it meets its connection with Cincinnati and the West.

Business men of experience predict, that one railroad with double track will not be adequate to the trade and travel of this route, once the western connections are established, and the country under fair way of development, and that the *James River and Ohio Canal* must eventually be completed to supply the wants of heavy freight. This water line, more recently known under the name of the "Virginia Canal," has long been in operation from tide water to Buchanan, Virginia, about fifty miles east of the Allegheny summit, a distance of 198 miles, leaving 203 miles yet to be completed to the Ohio river.

Lieut. Maury, in his able work "Physical Survey of Virginia," expresses the well sustained opinion "that the railroad will build the canal."

Repeated surveys of this water line demonstrate the feasibility of its construction, and the only doubts seem to hinge upon the supply of water on the summit throughout the year, without expensive reservoirs and aqueducts from a distance.

The West Virginia Central Railway is another line of improvement projected through the heart of the State, and under its amended charter granted in 1864, was intended to connect the Pennsylvania Central with the Chesapeake and Ohio Railroad. The points named upon the route are Brandonville, Preston Co., Mouth of Raccoon, Taylor county, Buckhannon, Upshur Co., and Charleston, Kanawha county, with privilege to change the location of its northern end, so as to follow the Monongahela river, Charleston still remaining a point at the other end. Upon either location, this road would aid in developing the rich belt of country embracing the largest portion of Elk and Monongahela valleys, famous for their wealth of coal and iron, magnificent timber, water power, and varied agricultural capabilities. Several counties upon the route are disposed to subscribe largely to the stock, and steps are being taken abroad to secure the residue of the capital required. The distance between the Chesapeake and Ohio, and the Baltimore and Ohio railroad, by the nearest practicable route is estimated at 125 miles.

Another North and South line, *the Monongalia and Lewisburg Railroad*, was chartered in 1865, but is not yet surveyed. The points named in the charter are Morgantown, Monongalia Co., Fairmont, Marion Co., Clarksburg, Harrison Co,, Buckhannon, Upshur Co., and Lewisburg, Greenbrier county. The construction of this road will develop at once the minerals, timber, the dairy and grazing resources, together with the immense water power of nearly the whole group of mountain counties. The prospects of this road were materially improved of late by its consideration at the hands of prominent capitalists in Pennsylvania, who are seeking a direct connection with the iron deposits of both Virginias, and the cotton fields of the South.

The Uniontown and West Virginia Railroad, lately chartered in Pennsylvania, and now being canvassed, will form the northern or connection link of the Monongalia and Lewisburg road.

An extension of the *Cumberland Valley Railroad* is contemplated from the Potomac river up the Valley of Virginia by way of Martinsburg.

The Potomac and Ohio Railroad, to connect the Ohio river south of Parkersburg with some point at or near Harper's Ferry, was chartered in 1869, but of its prospects of consummation nothing definite is yet ascertained. The same may be said of the *Cumberland, Moorefield & Broadway Railroad,* intended toconnect the North Branch of the Potomac, in Mineral county, West Virginia, with some point on the Virginia State line near Highland county, Virginia, probably with a view to a western or southern extension.

A direct railroad line from Washington City to Cincinnati has lately been surveyed through the central counties of West Virginia, crossing the Little Kanawha southwestward, near Glenville, in Gilmer county. This enterprise, though not chartered, is regarded as a "fixed fact" at no very distant time, and cannot possibly fail to traverse our State from East to West.

The Hempfield Railroad, connecting the Ohio Central with the Pittsburg and Connellsville road, has been in activity for several years past from Wheeling to Washington, Pa., a distance of 32 miles, of which 15 are in West Virginia.

Another short line from Steubenville, Ohio, to Pittsburg, now under construction, also crosses the Panhandle very near the Brooke and Hancock county line.

Should only one half of these iron roads be completed within the next ten years, there can be no doubt but that the time for profitable investment and location in West Virginia is NOW.

NAVIGATION.

The Ohio river, "the beautiful river" of early explorers, which forms the western boundary of the State for a distance of three hundred miles, is open to navigation with but rare interruptions from ice and low water, below the city of Wheeling, throughout the whole year. Daily, semi-weekly and tri-weekly steamers from that point and from Pittsburg to Cincinnati, Marietta and Parkersburg, and mail boats from Parkersburg to Charleston, by way of Gallipolis, Ohio, keep up constant communication between all the river landings in West Virginia, and between those points and the great markets in adjoining States. In a good stage of water, boats ascend the Monongahela as far up as Fairmont, the Little Kanawha to Glenville, and the Great Kanawha to the Falls, 35 miles above Charleston. The Ohio and Kanawha river navigation gives direct access to fifteen counties, placing seven others within one day's travel from its landings. By adding these to the eleven traversed by the Baltimore and Ohio Railroad, and ten more, accessible within 6 hours from the stations, it will be seen that the counties usually termed "remote," or inaccessible by easy routes, are reduced to a surprisingly small number.

"The Great Kanawha Navigation Company" is at present engaged in improving the river of that name by dredging, and in such other manner, as will furnish at least five feet of navigable water during the lowest stages of the Kanawha, from its mouth to Loup Creek Shoals, a distance of 95 miles, with privilege, upon certain contingencies to extend the said improvements up New river to the eastern line of the State. The works of the Company extend as far up the river as the Kanawha Salines, to which point navigation is uninterrupted in any stage of water.

The Little Kanawha Navigation Company is rapidly progressing in the improvement of the Little Kanawha river, from its mouth at Parkersburg, to the oil region at Burning Springs, a distance of 38 miles. Three locks and dams are required for this purpose, all of which are now under construction, and to be completed in 1870.

The immediate effects of this improvement will be:

1st, A large increase in the development of petroleum, which until now was materially thwarted by the uncertainty and irregularity of transportation.

2d, The end of rafting and floating of timber in the log, the erection of numerous saw mills, planing mills and similar institutions above the head of navigation, and the inducement of enterprise, population and improvement to the interior counties.

Once this enterprise in successful operation to Burning Springs, the salt, iron and lumber resources of the Little Kanawha basin, which embraces nearly 4000 square miles inclusively of all head waters, will soon induce an extension to Glenville or above, and solve the problem of the growth and prosperity of the city of Parkersburg, and intermediate points possessed of enterprise and favorable location.

Coal River was improved by locks and dams, and was navigated several years before the war, to the Peytona mines, 35 miles above its mouth. The reorganized Coal River Navigation Company has placed the improvement in good repair in view of large and steady developments. Little Coal river, by law a public highway, at present, is susceptible of improvement as far up as Ballardsville, the county seat of Boone.

On the Guyandotte river, improvements were in progress before the war, and dams built for some distance up, but neglected since and finally destroyed. The Guyandotte Navigation Company was rechartered in 1866, with privilege of completing the work within ten years.

The Big Sandy River, which divides West Virginia and Kentucky is navigated as far up as the lumbering town of Louisa, at the forks, but often practicable for many miles above.

The Monongahela is improved by slackwater from Pittsburg to within the West Virginia line.

The Chesapeake and Ohio Canal, from Cumberland to tide water at Georgetown, is fed by the Potomac river, and follows the West Virginia line from Cumberland to Harper's Ferry, a distance of over one hundred miles.

Of the natural capacity of inland streams, for boating and rafting, some information was already given in the chapter on Timber.

TURNPIKES AND COUNTRY ROADS.

The Cumberland road, formerly known as the "National road," a first-class macadamized turnpike, was once an important link of communication between the East and the West. Within this State its usefulness is now confined to the traffic of Ohio county and the adjoining section of Pennsylvania, with the city of Wheeling.

The Northwestern Turnpike, macadamized for the greater part of its length, connects Parkersburg with Winchester, Va., a distance of 230 miles, through nine counties. The grade nowhere exceeds four degrees, and the road is kept in tolerable repair, notwithstanding its proximity to the railroad West of the mountains, has somewhat diminished its utility. This road crosses the Alleghanies in Maryland, 40 miles East of the German settlement in the county of Preston.

The Staunton and Parkersburg Turnpike, also partially macadamized, extends between the two points which give its name, over a distance of 209 miles, through the counties of Wood, Ritchie, Gilmer, Lewis, Upshur, Randolph and Pocahontas, crossing the Alleghany ridge and State line in the northern corner of the latter county. Its steepest grade is said not to exceed three degrees, and although the road was severely abused during the war, and lacks a few bridges, it is still in tolerable repair, especially the western half.

The Kanawha and Lewisburg Turnpike, from Point Pleasant to White Sulphur Springs, is another East and West road, formerly much used, but in very inferior condition since the war.

Upward of thirty other Turnpikes of respectively from 10 to 100 miles in length, and none over five degrees of inclination, intersect the above East and West roads at different angles, and connect with each other all the counties North of the Great Kanawha valley. South of this line, roads are fewer and in worse repair, and in need of prompt and effective legislation. Under the old Virginia government, which held a three-fifth interest in all the chartered Turnpikes in the country, Superintendents were employed by the State to see to the repairs and the collection of tolls. The New State has relinquished all her right in those improvements, and turned them over for supervision and repair to the counties through which they respectively pass.

Q

County roads from 8 to 12 feet in width; and varying from 5 to 10 degrees of inclination, are constructed every where upon the petition of one or more settlers, praying for an outlet to the mill and to the county seat. There is not a county in the State without such neighborhood roads, and in many of them, one mile of road is found to every square mile of land, though it is but proper to add, that the quality is not generally in proportion to the quantity.

EDUCATION.

The educated and intelligent in West Virginia are so much like the educated and intelligent of every other civilized community, that the stranger, whose intercourse is confined to that class, can hardly realize the depth of popular ignorance, which was systematically nursed beneath this polished surface under the old State rule. Then the number of white adults, who could neither read nor write, amounted to over fifteen per cent. of the white population, while those who *could not spell*, but were never counted, probably represented 50 per cent. more.

FREE SCHOOLS.

All this is being changed now as rapidly as circumstances permit. Though remiss in regard to many other progressive measures, our Legislatures did not underrate the value of popular education, and a few months after the inauguration of the New State, a Free school law was elaborated, which was regarded as inferior to none in the States. Subsequent experience suggested a number of changes, which were successively adopted, without, however, having the effect of supplying the amount of intelligence, patient zeal, and public spirit required in the officers charged with the application of the system, in the rural districts especially. The jacket is yet too large for the boy, and a perfect fit necessarily a question of time.

From the Report of Prof. W. R. White, the State Superintendent of Free Schools, for 1868, it appears that there are 1825 school districts in the counties that have made their reports. Of these 519 are without school houses. Over 1200 school houses have been erected since the school system went into operation. These are valued at $668,817.92. The value of the land and other school property, such as furniture, apparatus, books, &c., swells this amount of $727,343.28. At least one half million dollars worth of school property, has been acquired since the organization of the State.

Of the 1306 school houses, 653 are frame, 51 brick, 7 stone and 595 log. Many of these log houses are a great improvement on the old style of log structures, affording very comfortable and appropriate school rooms. Furniture and apparatus are supplied to a large number of these houses. The libraries begin to show themselves, as well as other indications of progress in culture and intelligence. The average value of school houses is $483, the minimum value being $94, and the maximum $6000. The house now being built in Wellsburg will cost $25,000. It promises to be a model school house in every respect.

Three Union schools, twenty graded, and 1731 primary schools have been taught, which, with five grammar, and ten graded primary schools in the city of Wheeling, make the whole number of schools 1769. The number of youth is 130,898. Taking the returns from several counties, where the schools are in full operation, about sixty per cent. of the youth enrolled attend school, and about forty per cent. is the average daily attendance. These figures show an increase of nearly ten per cent. over last years report.

At the time of this writing the State Superintendent's Report for 1869 is not yet published; but the annual message of Gov. Stevenson refers to it as follows:

From the Report of the General Superintendent, it will be seen that the amount expended within that time for building purposes, was $264,995, being $20,609, more than was expended for the same purposes during the previous year.

The total amount expended for carrying on the schools, was $295,950, an increase over the expenditures of the previous year of $9,485,

The number of schools taught within the year was 2164, being an increase over the preceding year of 395.

The whole number of school houses built within the State up to the close of the school year, was 1708, the number erected during the year just past being 366.

The value of school property within the State at the present time is $956,112; increase in the value of property over the previous year $228,770.

The number of teachers employed during the year was 2,283, being 463 more than the year preceeding.

The enumeration of youth in the State, between the ages of six, and twenty-one, is shown to be 154,864; an increase over the enumeration of the previous year, of 2243.

The number of children attending school was 78,342; exceeding the number in the previous year by 24,618.

The permanent, or irreducible school fund, amounts at the present time to $231,200; the increase of the fund during the past year was 21,400."

The irreducible school fund referred to in the above report, is defined in article X of the State Constitution, page 27 of this volume, where the annual taxation for school purposes is also provided for.

NORMAL SCHOOLS.

The insufficiency of competent teachers within the State, was severely felt when the new system was first introduced, and at present a large proportion of schools are under the direction of able teachers from other States. To lessen our dependency in this respect, the Legislature provided for the establishment of Normal Schools for the special education of teachers. The principal institution of this class is located at Barboursville, in the county of Cabell, and its first branch at Fairmont. The Regents recommend that the West

Liberty Academy, in Ohio county, be placed upon the same footing with the other Normal Schools.

WEST VIRGINIA UNIVERSITY.

This institution occupies the seat of the former "Morgantown College" in the town of that name, situated on the banks of the Monongahela river, and noted for salubrity, morality and social refinement, no less than for the charm of its scenery. The University was partially endowed by a Congressional donation of Western lands, originally intended for, and applied to a State Agricultural College, which is now a part and branch of the higher Institution.

The three departments of the University, Literary, Scientific and Preparatory, embrace at this time the following: Mental and Moral Philosophy, English Literature, Astronomy and Physics, Mathematics and Military Tactics, Chemistry and Natural History, Ancient and Modern Languages, Agriculture and related subjects.

The number of students in the various departments for the current soolastic year, is 154, including 22 State cadets, two from each Senatorial district.

The University is already provided with the nucleus of a respectable library, physical and mathematical apparatus, and a Museum of natural and historical curiosities, which will be greatly augmented by contributions from the State Historical Society, lately founded under the auspices of the officers of the University.

The Governor's annual message thus refers to the condition and prospects of the Institution :

" Pupils are in attendance from nine different States and Territories; and in numbers greater than at any previous time. There is every prospect of a still larger increase, when the new University Hall, now being erected, shall have been completed.

So far, this institution has been more than ordinarily successful, and it is now exerting a wide influence for good throughout the State. Its success is due in a great measure to the good fortune of the Regents in securing the services of able and popular Professors, to the absence of political or sectarian influence in the management of the Institution and instruction of the students; and the sound judgment and persistent energy of its President. The University is fairly entitled to a place in the front rank of educational iustitutions, and merits continued encouragement and liberal support at your hands."

PRIVATE SCHOOLS.

In addition to the public institutions of learning, private Colleges, Academies, and schools of minor grades are found in almost every county in the State.

Most conspicuous and successful among these is Bethany College, in Brooke county, founded many years ago by the eminent Divine and scholar, Alex. Campbell, and extensively patronized by students from every part of the Union, intended for the ministry or the profession of teacher. Ever since its foundation this institution has occupied a distinguished position among the nurseries of all that is true, and great and good.

West Virginia College, at Flemington, Taylor county, was founded in 1866, by private enterprise, under highly respectable auspices, and is patronized by nearly one hundred students of both sexes.

The Academy of Mont de Chantal, near Wheeling, a Catholic Institute for young ladies, ranks high among schools of that class, and is open to pupils without distinction of religious persuasion.

Private schools, seminaries and academies of fair reputation, for both sexes, are flourishing at Wheeling, Wellsburg, Fairmont, Clarksburg, Parkersburg, Lewisburg, Charleston, Romney, Moorefield, Martinsburg, Shepherdstown, Charlestown, Harper's Ferry and other less populous county seats. Wheeling also boasts of a first class commercial college, and a public library of several thousand volumes.

COLORED SCHOOLS.

"The claims of the colored youth," says the State Superintendent, "have been duly considered, and I am gratified in saying that all agree in extending to them the greatest possible educational facilities. In places where their members will justify it, schools have been started, and their desire to learn has become very manifest. The Freedmen's Bureau has extended great help in the erection of school houses, for the use of colored people."

This assistance, amounting to $3,788.53, was distributed among thirteen towns of this State.

RELIGIOUS WORSHIP.

The early settlers of Western Virginia, notwithstanding their long seclusion from opportunities of religious worship and instruction, did not permit the seed of Faith to decay within their breasts. One of the first promptings of the growth and prosperity of a pioneer settlement, was the erection of a house of worship, a rude, hewed log meeting house, if nothing better, where, "in default of a regular pastor, the oldest inhabitant or 'the best scholar,'" conducted the prayer and expounded the Holy Writ. That much of this religious profession, up to this time, among the more illiterate classes, was little better than unthinking observance of the letter, without that intimate communion with the Deity which marks the intelligent Christian, cannot be questioned. Still, even viewed in this light, it is creditable as an indication of public opinion, which in West Virginia has always been decidedly conservative in matters of religion.

Neither in the moral and intellectual character of her clergy, nor in the number and appearance of her houses of worship, is West Virginia in arrear of any of her sister States similarly situated, and in this as well as in other channels of improvement, it is clearly apparent that the spirit of progress is on the move.

The Census of 1860, since which no official enumeration has taken place, gives the aggregate of the various denominations as follows:

Methodist, both branches, 149,550, with 508 churches; Episcopal 6675, with 24 churches; Baptists 55,749, with

169 churches; Presbyterians 37,660, with 90 churches; Union 9396, with 57 churches; Christian, (Campbellites) 3600, 19 churches; Dunker Baptists 2275, with 7 churches; Seven-day Baptists 750, with 4 churches; German Reformed 900, with 2 churches; Lutherans 5050, with 15 churches; Friends 135 with 1 church; Universalists 100, with 1 church.

The Roman Catholics are reported at 7950, but the R. C. Almanac for 1870, computes the aggregate number of members in the Diocese of Wheeling at 15,000, from which must be deducted about 1200 for three parishes in adjoining counties of Virginia, in all 35 churches, 9 chapels, 1 Orphan Asylum aud 1 Hospital.

Nearly all of the above denominations maintain a well organized system of Sunday Schools, in charge of zealous and efficient teachers.

The Young Mens' Christian Association, not sectarian in its character, and having for its object the mental, social and religious advancement of the young men, has organizations at Clarksburg, Moundsville, Parkersburg and Wheeling. Under their auspices, libraries and free reading rooms have been opened at Wheeling and Parkersburg.

LANDS AND FARMS.

TITLES.

The Commonwealth of Virginia, being one of the thirteen original States of the Federal Union, always held the individual right and title in the soil, and no United States or Congress lands were ever known within her limits. Applicants for entries were required to procure a warrant from the Register of the Land Office, paying for the same at the rate of 2½ cents per acre. The cost of surveying and patenting varied, according to size and shape of the tract, from 2½ to 5 cents, making the total cost of State land from 5 to 7½ cents per acre. The entry or location of the land was entirely at the option and risk of the patentee, and upon the principle of *caveat emptor*, no responsibility rested upon the Commonwealth, in case of interference with tracts previously granted. The State conveyed such title as she had, and nothing more.

In this manner the greater portion of the public lands was patented in tracts of from 50 acres to 500,000 acres, in early days, when danger from hostile Indians, and other inconveniences from a state of wilderness, did not admit of accurate and protracted surveying, and careful marking of boundaries.

From these causes and subsequent conflicting legislation in regard to forfeitures, tax sales, &c., much litigation arose, which seriously damaged the reputation of land titles in the old State.

During the decade preceding the war, however, this evil was materially checked by remedial legislation, and the limit of ten years for the perfection of title by actual possession, also tended to reduce litigation. One of the first steps of the new State government, was to stop the further entering and patenting of lands, by abolishing the Land Office forever. Practical legislation for the settlement of disputed titles within a few years, is now under consideration, and will probably be adopted.

In the meantime, no stranger seeking a home, or profitable investment, need to shun West Virginia lands, of which several millions of acres, in responsible private hands, may be obtained with titles as perfect as the United States grant to their own public domain. In no State of the Union, may real estate be bought with perfect safety, without consulting the public records or legal assistance, and when this simple precaution is observed in West Virginia, fraud or deception will not occur in one case out of a thousand. To the large capitalists contemplating investment here, advice in these pages is entirely superfluous. Parties at the head of from twenty to one hundred thousand dollars generally know how to get the worth of their money. As for the immigrant of moderate means, without friends to advise him, he may obviate every risk by purchasing through or with the assistance of a respectable land agency or legal counsel, or by learning something of the history of the people and locality by a little personal acquaintance, before closing the transaction. Instances where parties have been defrauded by bad titles purchased here, on the spot, are equally as rare as in any adjoining States, and much more so than in Missouri, at present.

Parties purchasing tracts in the interior or border counties of 5,000 acres and upward, may generally expect to find a few adverse occupants upon them, who, if not removed by the seller, will have to be compromised with. Some of them who have occupied their improvements for ten consecutive years under color of title, hold under the statute of limitation, and will have to be "let alone," or bought off, if their land is needed. Other occupants, without color of title, are simply *squatters*, and liable to an action of ejectment. But an amicable arrangement with these settlers will always be found the most expedient course, besides being the most just. The improvements and roads, however rude, have added to the actual value of the land, and if wanted, should be paid for at an equitable rate. An offer to do this, and courteous treatment, will seldom fail to effect the desired result. Land suits should always be avoided in West Virginia, even at a sacrifice, by parties not in possession of a full purse, superhuman patience, and a long lease of life.

LEASES.

Immigrants not willing or able to purchase lands, may find an opportunity to lease improvements in the older settlements, for a third or half share of the crops, or for a stipulated cash rent. Where the owner furnishes the seed and team, the tenants share is proportionally less.

Leases on unimproved land are usually granted upon the following terms: The tenant agrees to build a house and outhouses, plant an orchard, and to clear and fence so many acres within so many years. and to have the exclusive use and benefit of the same during that time, at the expiration of which the improvements revert to the owner, unless the contract provides, that the tenant shall have the option to purchase the land and improvements at a stated price at the end of his lease. The latter clause brings the acquisition of lands within reach of immigrants of very limited means, with the advantage of holding the land, as it were, on probation, until they are satisfied with the adaptedness of the country to their wants and circumstances, without being in the meantime burdened and disquieted by pecuniary liabilities.

TERMS OF PURCHASE.

Nearly all the cheaper lands in the State may be obtained upon easy terms of credit. The usual conditions are from $\frac{1}{3}$ to $\frac{1}{2}$ cash; balance in several annual payments. There are not a few land owners who will require only a nominal cash payment, or none at all, from actual settlers, in order "to make a start." On improved lands one-half cash is generally expected on their vacant estates; balance payable in 1 to 3 years, unless the owner intends to remove to a distance, and needs his means to pay for a new home, in which case the credit is shortened or altogether dispensed with. The legal rate of interest on deferred payments is six per cent.

VALUATION AND PRICE.

The Census of 1860, reports the number of farms in West Virginia at 28,349, classed as follows:

From	3 to 10	acres, 1266	farms.
"	10 to 20	" 2955	"
"	20 to 50	" 9030	"
"	50 to 100	" 7653	"
"	100 to 500	" 7438	"
"	500 to 1000	" 246	"
"	1000 and over,	65	"

At the rate of progression of population, the number of farms in the State, at this time, should be near 40,000. The total value of land and buildings i. e. unimproved land and farms, is stated in the Auditor's Report for 1869, at $81,358,232, and that of town lots and buildings at $14,826,256. Total valuation of real estate, $96,184,488. But as these figures are based upon the Assessor's returns, from 50 to 150 per cent. should be added, in order to reach the true cash value, which owners, disposed to sell, are willing to take. During the prevalence of war taxes, now entirely paid up, the people contracted the habit of largely undervaluing their land, and the Assessors, being landholders themselves, connived at the deception.

Since the abatement of the mineral excitement, the land market has relapsed into a normal condition, and in many localities prices are not higher at present than when gold was at par. Landholders are beginning to appreciate the policy of selling off a portion of their estate, in order to improve and enhance the remainder, and are holding out unprecedented inducements to immigration, by colonies and single families.

Wild lands, in sections of the State not accessible by railroads and navigable streams, no matter how rich in minerals or timber, are now offered at low farming prices, and in tracts to suit purchasers. Rich, rough, declivitous mountain lands, with a small proportion of arable surface, may be had at from 50 to 75 cents per acre, in the counties of Fayette, Pocahontas, Clay, Tucker, Nicholas, Randolph, Raleigh, Logan, Wyoming, McDowell and Webster, which are named here in the order of their official valuation. Such lands may some day be developed for their timber, and then profitably used as sheep pasture. *But moderately hilly and table lands in the same counties, of sufficient quality to afford a comfortable existence to an industrious family on one hundred acres*, command from $1 to $3 per acre. Among this class of lands there are large tracts that would command $10 per acre now, if situated within two hour's travel from a line of transportation. The lowest price above named is asked for large tracts, if taken entire, of from 5000 to 20,000 acres, and even 40,000 to 50,000 acres. For smaller and piched lots an advance is of course expected.

The term "Improved land," is assumed to apply to farms of which from one-tenth to one-half or more, is under cultivation, and the balance in timber.

BRIEF SKETCH OF COUNTIES.

BARBOUR.—Tygart's Valley river. Several turnpikes. Rich'Mountain on the east. Land rich, rolling and hilly. Well improved farms. Coal and iron. Improved land $10 to 20, unimproved $2 to 6 per acre. Postoffices 14.

PHILIPPI C. H,—By turnpike from Clarksburg 20 m.; from Webster Station 14 m. Favorable location on the river. Weekly paper, " The Old Flag."

BERKELEY.—Potomac river and canal, B. & O. R. R., and turnpikes. North Mountain. A fair proportion of bottom and smooth valley land. Good improvements. Some anthracite coal. Improved land $15 to 100, unimproved $5 to 15. Postoffices 13.

MARTINSBURG, C. H.—101 miles from Baltimore, a wealthy and thriving town. 3000 inhabitants. Manufactures. Banks: First National, capital $50,000. Weekly papers, "The Berkeley Union," "New Era," and "Valley Star."

BOONE.—Coal and Little Coal rivers. Turnpike from Kanawha river. Rich hilly land; narrow but fertile valleys. Large veins of bituminous and cannel coal, mined at Peytona and other points. Improved land $5 to 15, unimproved $1 to 5 per acre. Postoffices 5.

BALLARDSVILLE, C. H. (address Boone C. H.)—A new place, 20 miles from Ches. & Ohio R. R.

BRAXTON.—Elk river, Birch river. Location of West Va. Central R. R., turnpikes. Fertile country, with a variety of surface, good proportion of smooth upland. Improvements medium. Coal, iron, salt; gas and burning springs. Improved land $5 to 15, unimproved in large and small tracts $2 to $5 per acre. Postoffices 9.

SUTTON, C. H.—60 miles from Balt. & O. R. R., 90 m. from Ches. & O. R. R. A small place, but well located. Accessible from Clarksburg via Weston.

BROOKE.—Ohio river and railroad. Highly improved farms. Bottom and rolling land. Abundance of coal. Farming, wool growing and manufacturing. Improved land $30 to 100 per acre. Postoffices 5. Good roads.

WELLSBURG, C. H.—An old and wealthy town, 16 m. above Wheeling. Weekly paper "Wellsburg Herald." Banks: First National, capital $100,000. Bethany College 8 m. distant by turnpike.

CABELL—Ohio river, Ches. & O. R. R., Guyandotte and Mud rivers. Large Ohio bottoms, well improved. Interior hilly but rich. German settlements. Coal and iron. Improved land $30 to 100, unimproved $2 to 10 per acre, according to proximity to the Ohio river and railroad.

BARBOURSVILLE, C. H. (P. O. address, Cabell C. H.)—At the junction of Mud and Guyandotte rivers. Marshall College, the State Normal School, is situated in this vicinity. Weekly paper, "The Cabell Co. Press."

CALHOUN.—Little Kanawha river, West Fork and Steer creek. Turnpike. Rich, hilly and rolling land. Improved lands $5 to 15, unimproved $2 to 5 per acre, large tracts at lower prices. Postoffices 5.

GRANTSVILLE, C. H.—The county seat for the present; ARNOLDSBURG claims the court house. Both very small places; reached from the Balt. & O. R. R. by Ellenboro.

CLAY.—Elk river, location W. Va. Central R. R. Large bituminous and cannel coal seams; iron and probably salt. Large gas springs. Surface broken, river bottoms narrow. Large tracts of wild lands with minerals and good timber at $1 to 2 per acre, improved lands $5 to 15 per acre. Postoffices 2.

MARSHALL, C. H.—About 50 miles above Charleston and Ches. & O. R. R. P. O. address Clay C. H.

DODDRIDGE.—Middle Island creek and Hughes' river. B. & O. R. R., Northwestern and other turnpikes. Surface rolling and hilly, average bottoms. Coal, bituminous shale, iron. Good soil and valuable timber. Unimproved lands $3 to 15, improved $7,50 to 20 per acre, mostly in small and medium sized tracts.

WEST UNION, C. H.—600 inhabitants, 55½ miles from Parkersburg, 327 from Baltimore. Other railroad stations, Tollgate, Greenwood, Central, Smithton, and Long Run. St. Clara colony, a German settlement, 15 miles south, on Cove creek.

FAYETTE.—New river, Kanawha and Gauley rivers, Ches. & Ohio R. R. and turnpike. Big Sewell and Gauley Mountains and Cotton Hill. Kanawha Falls. Surface monntainous and hilly, but rich. Coal and iron. Improved lands $5 to 20, unimproved $1 to 5, Large tracts on hand. Grazing, wool growing, fruit and timber. Postoffices 10.

FAYETTEVILLE, C. H.—6 miles from railroad.

GILMER.—Little Kanawha river, Steer, Cedar and Leading creeks. Staunton and Parkersburg turnpike and others. Rich, hilly surface, with some fine bottom farms. Coal, salt and iron. Burning springs. Steamboat yard. Land in small and large tracts, unimproved $2 to 5, improved $7 to 15 per acre. Postoffices 10. Foreign settlements on Sand Fork.

GLENVILLE, C. H.—300 inhabitants, 33 miles from Balt. & O. R. R., at West Union.

GRANT.—North and South branches of the Potomac, Patterson's Creek, N. W. Turnpike and others. Alleghany mountains. Surface mountainous with smooth valleys and table lands. Coal and iron. Improved lands $10 to 25, unimproved in large and small tracts $1.25 to 5 per acre. Postoffices 9.

GRANT, C. H.—Centrally located, but not yet built, about 30 miles from New Creek station. Petersburg, small town on the South Branch.

GREENBRIER.—Greenbrier, New and Meadow rivers. Ches. & O. R. R. and turnpikes. Alleghany and Greenbrier mountains. Smooth, rolling hills and low mountains and table lands. Farms highly improved. Grain, grazing, and wool growing. Mean elevation above tide water, 1500 feet, but mild climate. Improved land $10 to 50, unimproved including some broken surface $3 te 5 per acre. Postoffices 13.

LEWISBURG, C. H.—A very old settled, wealthy town in a beautiful location. Weekly paper, "The Phœnix."

HANCOCK.—Ohio river, near Steubenville & Pittsburgh R. R. The most northern county in the State. Similar in soil to the adjoining county of Brooke, with somewhat more broken surface. A small but highly improved and thrifty county, principally devoted like the other Panhandle and adjoining Pennsylvania counties, to sheep and wool growing. Improved land $30 to 100, unimproved $6 to 30. Very little land for sale. Good roads and 5 postoffices.

FAIRVIEW, C. H.—Other places of note: New Cumberland and Hollyday's Cove. Monthly paper: "Hollyday's Cove Little Joker." Weekly paper, "Hancock Co. Courier."

HAMPSHIRE.—Potomac river and branches, B. & O. R. R., North river and Cacapon mountains. Northwestern and other turnpikes. High mountains, and wide fertile valleys, well improved. Grain farming. grazing and wool growing. Unimproved mountain lands $1,25 to 5, farms $15 to 50 per acre. Postoffices 19.

Natural curiosities: Ice mountain, Hanging Rock, Tea Table, Capon Springs.

ROMNEY, C. H.—On the South Branch and N. W. Turnpike. Is reached from Green Spring depot and from New Creek station, Balt. & Ohio R. R.. Small but thriving town. Bank. Weekly, paper, "The South Branch Intelligencer." Railroad stations, Green Spring Run and Little Cacapon.

HARRISON.—West Fork and branches. B. & O. Railroad, N. W. Turnpike and others. Rolling and hilly, with expansive valleys, rich soil and well improved farms. First county in the State in value of live stock. Large seams of bituminous coal now developed; also cannel coal and iron ore. Salt was formerly manufactured at Clarksburg. Postoffices 23. Improved land $10 to $50, unimproved $5 to $15 per acre.

CLARKSBURG, C. H.—From Baltimore 301 miles, Parkersburg, 82. Population 1500. The town is beautifully located on a plateau at the junction of Elk creek and the West Fork of the Monongahela river, and contains much solid wealth, and unsurpassed natural elements of growth and prosperity, which are as yet but partially developed. Merchant's National Bank, capital $100,000. Weekly papers: "National Telegraph" and "Conservative." U. S. District Court.

HARDY.—South Branch of Potomac and branches. Mountain land of varied surface and soil, and wide fertile valleys. A rich farming and grazing county. Coal and iron. Postoffices 11. Improved land $10 to 25, unimproved $1.25 to 5, in large or small lots.

MOOREFIELD, C. H.—Forty miles from New Creek Station by Turnpikes. Population 600. Weekly paper, the Moorefield Advertiser.

Natural curiosities: Regurgitary Springs, Lost river and Devil's Garden.

JACKSON.—Ohio river, Sand and Mill creeks. Several Turnpikes. Surface hilly and rolling, and good sized bottoms on all the principal streams. Soil generally rich, and farms in average condition. A fair farming and grazing county. Improved land $7 to 20, unimproved, $3 to 7 per acre. Postoffices 16.

RIPLEY, C. H.—A small but active place, 16 miles from the Ohio river. Weekly paper, the "West Virginia News," and "Cottageville Weekly Press."

Principal landings on the river, Ravenswood and Ripley Landing.

JEFFERSON.—Potomac and Shenandoah rivers. B. & O. Railroad, and Winchester Railroad. A thickly settled, highly improved and wealthy county. Large population. Level and undulating limestone land. First county in asssessed, and unquestionably first in actual value of real estate, and in the production of wheat and corn. Good Turnpike roads, and 11 Post-offices, of which 3 are railroad stations.

SHEPHERDSTOWN, C. H.—On the Potomac, North of the Railroad. A rising town, population 2000. Weekly paper: "Shepherdstown Register." Railroad Stations, Harper's Ferry, Duffiield, Kearneysville.

Charlestown, the former county seat, is situated on the Winchester Railroad, in the center of the county, 8 miles from Harper's Ferry. Weekly paper: "The Spirit of Jefferson."

KANAWHA.—Great Kanawha, Elk, Coal and Pocatalico rivers. Chesapeake & Ohio Railroad. Surface in part very hilly and rolling, with a fair proportion of bottom in the valleys. Farming and grazing land. A good portion of the virgin land is rough, but generally fertile, and all of it underlaid with coal and other minerals, principally iron and salt, (see chapter on Mineral Resources.) Improved land not held for mineral purposes, $40 to 75, unimproved $3 to 10 per acre. Several small towns along the Kanawha river, and in all 18 Postoffices, German settlement.

CHARLESTON, C. H., (P. O. address, Kanawha C. H.) —On the Railroad location and at the mouth of Elk river, 60 miles from the Ohio river. Population 2500. The State Capital was located here by the Legislature in 1869, but the location is yet open to repeal. An old town of Southern style, but admirably situated for trade and manufactures, which up to this time were nearly confined to the article of salt. The wealth of the town, large as it is, consists principally in lands and mineral interests, without a sufficiency of cash capital for extensive developments. Weekly papers: the "West Virginia Journal," and "Kanawha Republican." Merchant's Bank, and Bank of the West. U. S. District Court.

LEWIS.—West Fork of the Monongahela. Staunton and Parkersburg Turnpike, and on one of the proposed Railroad routes South. Surface hilly and rolling, uniformly fertile. Average bottoms on the principal streams. Farms well improved, and principally devoted to grazing. Coal and iron. Postoffices 16. Improved land $6 to 20. Unimproved, in small and moderate sized tracts, $2 to 10 per acre.

WESTON, C. H.—Population 1000. 23 miles from Clarksburg. A well located, growing town, containing much solid wealth. Weekly paper: the "Weston Democrat." Bank: the First National, capital $200,000.

The West Virginia Hospital for the Insane is located here, and nearly half completed. It is a large and first class structure, accommodating at present 202 patients.

LOGAN.—Guyandotte and Big Sandy rivers. Surface quite hilly, with narrow bottoms. Soil generally rich, and productive to the very summits. Well adapted to grazing, and particularly to sheep-husbandry. Winters mild and short. Great variety of native herbage. Logan claims to rank first in the production of Ginseng. Abundance of coal, and iron. Burning springs on Sandy river. Indications of salt. Magnificent timber. Improved land $5 and 10, unimproved, $1 to 5 per acre. Large tracts in the market. Turnpike and 5 Postoffices.

LOGAN C. H.—On Guyandotte river, 50 miles from the Chesapeake and Ohio Railroad at Charleston or Coalsmouth.

LINCOLN.—Coal, Guyandotte and Mud rivers. A new county taken from Boone, Cabell and Logan, and very similar in surface and soil. Valleys are wider than in Logan, and owing to the mineral developments lands are held at somewhat higher prices. Improved land $5 to 15, unimproved, in tracts of from 100 to 10,000 acres, $1.25 to 3 per acre. The large coal seams of Coal and Elk river extend entirely through Lincoln county, to Cabell and Logan. No county seat established yet. Distance from northern end of Lincoln county to Chesapeake and Ohio Railroad, about 8 miles. Postoffices, 8.

MARION.—Monongahela and Tygarts Valley rivers. B. & O. R. R. and on the proposed route of the

Uniontown & West Virginia R. R., several turnpike roads. Much of the surface smooth and rolling; fertile soil. Well improved farms, extensive grazing and considerable industrial activity. The best of bituminous coal, iron, sand for glass manufacturing. Improved land $15 to 50, unimproved, almost everywhere valuable for timber purposes, $5 to 12 per acre. Postoffices 20.

FAIRMONT, C. H.—On the river and railroad, 302 m. from Baltimore, 77 m. from Wheeling. A thriving town, in a pleasant and commanding situation. Weekly paper, "The West Virginian." Bank: First National.

McDOWELL.—Tug Fork of Big Sandy river. 60 miles from Ches. & Ohio R. R. at Gauley Bridge. This county was recently taken from Logan, which it resembles exactly in surface and soil. Much of the land is owned by non-residents and titles were formerly involved, which retards development. Improved land $5 to 10; unimproved, in very large tracts, if desired, at $1.25 to 2.50 per acre.

PERRYILLE, C. H.—Not much improved yet. Besides this, there is one other Postoffice, called, "Snake Root."

MARSHALL.—Ohio river, Grave creek, B. & O. R. R. Fair proportion of bottom lands, balance rolling and hilly, none very rough, soil uniformly rich. Farms highly improved and well cultivated. Large grain crops. Improved land $15 to 100, unimproved, in small tracts $5 to 10 per acre. Good roads and 15 postoffices.

MOUNDSVILLE, C. H.—On the river and railroad. 368 miles from Baltimore, 11 miles from Wheeling. A growing, well located town. State Penitentiary. Weekly paper, "The National."

Curiosites: Indian mound.

MASON.—Ohio and Great Kanawha rivers. A wealthy county; with nearly 80 miles of river front, and extensive bottoms, all well improved. Rolling, fertile hill land. Coal mined at West Columbia; salt manufactured at Hartford City and N. Haven; nails at Mason City. Improved lands $15 to 100, unimproved, to be had in small lots only, $4 to 7 per acre. Branch railroad contemplated from the Ches. & O. R. R. Passable turnpike roads and 19 postoffices.

Point Pleasant, C. H.—At the mouth of Kanawha river. One of the most advantageous locations on the Ohio river, and susceptible of extensive improvement. Weekly papers, "The Mason Co. Journal." and "Point Pleasant Register." Banks, Merchants National Bank, capital $180,000.

MERCER.—Between Flat Top and East River mountains. New river and Bluestone river. A hilly and rolling surface, gradually sloping up to both mountains. Fertile grain and grazing land, principally limestone. Improved land $10 to 25, unimproved, in good sized and small tracts $1.50 to 5 per acre. Postoffices 7.

Princeton, C. H.—A small town about 30 m. from Ches. & O. R. R.

MINERAL.—Potomac river, New and Patterson's creek. Alleghany and Nobly mountains. Balt. & O. R. R. Lately taken from Hampshire and of similar surface and soil. Mountains high with but little table land, valleys wide, fertile and well improved. Coal, mined extensively for Eastern market. Iron ore. Improved lands $20 at 30; unimproved, according to surface, $1.50 to 10 per acre.

New Creek, C. H.—On the the railroad 201 m. from Baltimore. Population 500, favorably situated and improving. Weekly paper, "Mineral Co. Gazette." Piedmont, 5 m. west of New Creek, has a larger population, and is rapidly progressing in trade, mining, etc.

MONONGALIA.—Monongahela and Cheat river. Laurel Hill to the East. Varied surface, moderately broken, with smooth and fertile valleys, under good cultivation. Farming, grazing and wool growing. Coal and iron ore. Improved lands $10 to 40; unimproved, principally in the western portion of the county $3 to 10, Several turnpike roads, and 21 postoffices. Location of projected railroads.

Morgantown, C. H.—16 miles by turnpike and stage from Fairmont; population 1100. A pleasant and wealthy place. Weekly papers, "Morgantown Post," and "Constitution." Banks: The Merchants National Bank of West Virginia, capital $110,000. Some manufacturing. The West Virginia University is here. (See chapter on Education.)

MONROE.—New river and Greenbrier river. Ches. & Ohio R. R. A fine farming and grazing county, very much like Greenbrier county, which is adjacent. Old, well improved farms. Blue, Red and Sweet Sulphur Springs. Improved land $10 to 30, unimproved mountain land $3 to 5 per acre. Postoffices 18.

UNION, C. H.—Population 600, about 15 miles from Ches. & Ohio R. R. Weekly paper, "The Union Register."

MORGAN.—Potomac river, canal, B. & O. R. R. Cacapon mountain. Mountainous surface with several fertile valleys. Good grazing and dairy land; not extensively improved. Coal and iron. Good timber. Improved lands $10 to 60, unimproved $2 to 10 per acre. Postoffices 10.

BERKELEY SPRINGS, C. H.—A small town, 2½ m. from St. John's Run station, and noted for its mineral springs (see chapter under that head) and attractive scenery. Weekly paper, "The Morgan Mercury." Railroad stations in the county: Cacapon Depot, Cherry Run Depot, Hancock, and St. John's Run. 128 miles from Baltimore, 251 from Wheeling.

NICHOLAS.—Gauley river and branches. Birch Mountain. Turnpikes. Hilly, rolling, and glade, or table land, and some good valleys. Nearly all rich land and adapted to grazing and mixed farming. A large proportion of unimproved land, in large or small tracts, at $1 to 3 per acre, improved at from $5 to 15 per acre. Coal, iron and appearances and other minerals. Postoffices 5.

SUMMERSVILLE, C. H. (P. O. address Nicholas C. H.) —On the Ganley bridge turnpike about 30 m. from Ches. & Ohio R. R.

OHIO.—Ohio river and the Baltimore & Ohio Railroad. Land rolling and hilly with large bottoms on the Ohio river and Wheeling Creek. Rich soil, highly cultivated. Grain, fruit and wine, and wool growing. Manufactures, coal and iron. Ohio is the first county in amount of real estate and the second in the nnmber of sheep, coming within a few hundred of Brooke county, which is the first in this line. Unimproved lands not in market, improved from $20 to 300 per acre.

WHEELING, C. H.—River and R. R. Population 18,-006. Temporary capital of the State. A compactly built and well improved city, in want of room for expansion. Extensive wholesale trade, and manufacturing (see page 251.) Four National Banks, aggregate capital $1,100,000. Two State or private banks, aggregate capital $320,000. Newspapers: "Daily and Weekly, "The Wheeling Intelligencer" and "Wheeling Register." German weeklies: "The Patriot," and "The Arbeiter-freund.". U. S. Dist. Court and Custom House.

PENDLETON.—Alleghany and Shenandoah mountains. South Branch of Potomac river. Turnpikes and projected railroad line. Notwithstanding its elevated and secluded position, this county ranks high in the production of grain as well as live stock. Surface in part mountainous, with many smooth valleys and table lands. Well worked and highly improved farms on the highest levels. Unimproved lands, in extensive tracts if desired, at $1.25 to 5 per acre, improved $6 to 15 per acre. Postoffices 10.

FRANKLIN, C. H.—An old settled town, 35 or 40 miles from the Chesapeake and Ohio Railroad at Buffalo Gap. Pennsylvania German settlements in several parts of the county.

PLEASANTS.—Ohio river and Turnpike roads. Middle Island creek, Cow creek and French creek. Oil Belt runs entirely through the county. Fine Ohio bottom lands. Inland hills of good surface, and in part very rich. Improved lands $10 to 100, unimproved in small tracts, $5 to 10 per acre. Postoffices 6.

ST. MARY'S, C. H.—500 inhabitants. On the Ohio river. Fine location, with much room for improvement. 27 miles from Parkersburg.

POCAHONTAS.—Alleghany and Greenbrier mountains and Greenbrier river. Head waters of Gauley. Staunton and Parkersburg, and other Turnpike roads. Location of the Monongalia and Lewisburg Railroad. Great variety of surface and soil. Rough mountains, smooth table lands and wide, fertile valleys, with well improved grazing farms. Unimproved lands, in tracts to suit purchasers, of average soil and surface, $1.25 to 5, and improved $6 to 25 per acre. Coal and superior iron ore. Saltpetre and sulphur springs. Postoffices 11.

HUNTERSVILLE, C. H.—On Knapp's creek, on a commanding plateau, 1500 feet above tide water. About 40 miles from Chesapeake & Ohio Railroad at White Sulphur Springs.

PRESTON.—B. & O. Railroad,and location of the West Virginia Central Railroad. Northwestern and other Turnpike roads. Laurel, Cheat and Alleghany mountains. Cheat river and tributaries, and head branches of Tygart's Valley river. Notwithstanding its broken surface and narrow valleys, a rich and productive county. Mountains, with some glades and table lands, and rich low hills and fertile slopes. Abundance of bituminous and cannel coal, superior iron ore, (see chapter on Minerals.) Unimproved lands in small and moderately sized tracts, $2.50 to 10, unimproved, $7 to 20 per acre. Postoffices 24. Several German settlements.

KINGWOOD, C. H.—An ancient place, 8 miles from B. & O. Railroad. Very handsomely located. Population 800. First National Bank: capital $100,000. Weekly paper: "Preston County Journal."

Railroad Stations: Cranberry Summit, Rowlesburg, Tunnelton, Independence and Newburg. Tunnelton is 119 miles from Wheeling, and 260 miles from Baltimore.

PUTNAM.—Kanawha and Pocatalico rivers. Chesapeake & Ohio Railroad, and on the route of the projected branch to Point Pleasant. Fine bottom lands on both sides of Kanawha river. Some moderately smooth and rich rolling land, and some rougher hills.

Farms generally in good condition, and held nearly at Ohio river prices, say from $30 to 75. Unimproved, $2 to 10 per acre. Coal mining at Raymond City.

WINFIELD, C. H.—A new town, eligibly located on the Kanawha river. Weekly paper published at Buffalo: the "Buffalo Independent."

RALEIGH.—New river and head of Coal river, C. & O. Railroad and Turnpike roads. Flat Top and Great Cherry Pond mountains. Mountain land rough and stony, but much of the Coal river section is rolling, with a large extent of nearly level land known as the Marshes of Coal. Large tracts of wild lands, some with accessible timber, at from $1 to 3 per acre, improved lands, $6 to 15. Coal and iron. Postoffices 8.

BECKLEY, (Postoffice address Raleigh C. H.)—On Piney crreek and Turnpike, 24 miles from C. and O. Railroad.

RANDOLPH.—Rich, Cheat and Alleghany mountains. Tygart's Valley and Cheat rivers. Staunton and Parkersburg, and other Turnpikes. Location of the Monongalia and Lewisburg Railroad. A large county with an unusual proportion of rich valley and smooth upland, main Cheat and Shaver's mountain being the only rough ridges. Large tracts of timbered lable land on tho head of Cheat, Greenbrier and Valley rivers at from $1 to 2.50 per acre, improved mountain land $4 to 10. Tygart valley bottom land, with a portion of adjacent hill, $20 to 50 per acre. These farms were well improved before the war, and are fast being repaired. Coal and iron, and traces of lead. Postoffices 13.

BEVERLY, C. H.—About 500 inhabitants. Centrally located, in one of the widest parts of Tygart's Valley. Distance by Turnpike roads, by way of Philippi, 50 miles to Clarksburg, 44 miles to Webster Station. To Buffalo Gap, Chesapeake and Ohio Railroad, by the Staunton Turnpike, 79 miles.

RITCHIE.—Baltimore & Ohio Railroad. Northwestern, Staunton and Parkersburg, and other Turnpike roads. North and South forks of Hughes' river.

Oil Belt crosses the western end. Surface hilly and rolling. Fertile, winding valleys. Improvements generally good. Coal, Asphaltum and Petroleum.

Railroad Stations: Pennsboro, Ellenboro, Cornwaltis, Cairo, Petroleum, and 16 Postoffices.

HARRISVILLE, C. H., (Postoffice address, Ritchie C. H.)—On Harrisville and Salem Turnpike, 5 miles from Ellenboro Station. Population 500. A neat village, very pleasantly situated. Weekly paper: the "West Virginia Star."

A railroad, 14 miles long, is constructed from Cairo Station to the asphaltum mines on McFarland's run.

ROANE.—Reedy creek, Spring creek, West Fork of Little Kanawha, and head of Pocatalico river. Gilmer and Ravenswood Turnpike. Surface hilly, with some average sized valleys, and low flat hills in the southern portion of the county, and nearly all of it exceedingly rich. Unimproved land in moderate sized tracts, with splendid timber, $3.50 to 5, improved $7.50 to 15 per acre. Small veins of coal, traces of iron. Postoffices 9.

SPENCER, C. H.—A small, new place, in a pleasant situation in Spring creek valley, 35 miles from Ravenswood, on the Ohio river, 20 miles from the Little Kanawha, and 25 miles from the location of the W. Va., Central Railroad on Elk river.

TAYLOR.—Baltimore and Ohio Railroad. Tygart's Valley river and branches. Northwestern Turnpike, and other roads. A small, but highly improved county. Surface rolling and hilly, with an large proportion of arable surface. Coal and iron. Abundance of roads, and 8 Postoffices.

PRUNTYTOWN, C. H.—On the Northwestern Turnpike, 3 miles from Fetterman station, on the Baltimore and Ohio Railroad, population 800.

Railroad Stations: Grafton, on the Valley river, junction of main stem and Parkersburg Branch. A growing town 104 miles from Parkersburg, 100 miles from Wheeling, 270 miles from Baltimore. Webster, Flemington and Thornton. Weekly papers: the "Echo" at Pruntytown, "The Virginian," at Fetterman.

TUCKER.—Alleghany and Cheat mountains, and Laurel Hill. Cheat river and branches. A small county. Rough mountain land, varied with rolling upland and table land, of excellent soil. Valleys generally narrow but fertile. Cultivated surface small. Owing to scantiness of roads, land sells here below intrinsic value. Unimproved, generally welll timbered, from $1 to 5, in lots to suit, improved, $5 to 15 per acre. Postoffices 8:

St. George, C. H.—A new village, about 25 miles from Rowlesburg Station, by Cheat river valley.

TYLER.—Ohio river, Middle Island creek. Several Turnpike roads, southern line 3 miles from railroad. Fine Ohio bottom lands, well improved. Inland surface hilly, with many bottom and rolling farms on Middle Island creek and branches. Soil generally rich. Unimproved land $3.50 to 7, improved $10 to 100. Postoffices 13.

Middlebourne, C. H.—Population 500. On Turnpike 10 miles from Sistersville, on the Ohio river, 55 miles below Wheeling.

UPSHUR.—Buckhannon Fork of Tygart's Valley river, and head branches of Elk river. Location of the Monongalia and Lewisburg Railroad, and possibly, of the West Virginia Central. Staunton and Parkersburg Turnpike and other roads. This county forms the first bench on the gradual ascent toward the mountains, the Buckhannon Fork level being probably 250 feet above the head valleys of Elk creek and Stone Coal creek, immediately adjacent. Diversified surface, in part rough, with a fair proportion rich, undulating, and gently sloping; embracing some fine grazing table land toward head waters. Bituminous and cannel coal, iron ore. Some well improved and productive farms rate at $15 to 25 per acre, mountain farms 5 to te 10 per acre, unimproved lands, in small or good sized tracts, 2 to 4; and for less if bought under quit claim deed. Postoffices 10.

Buckhannon, C. H.—A well located little town, 28 miles from Clarksburg, by Turnpike. Weekly paper: "The Buckhannon Advocate."

WAYNE.—Chesapeake and Ohio Railroad; Ohio, Twelve Pole and Big Sandy rivers. Kentucky line. Large Ohio river bottoms, finely improved. Interior lands hilly and similar to the adjoining county of Cabell, and uniformly rich. Large production in proportion to cultivated surface. Bituminous and cannel coal abundant. Roads scant. Postoffices 10.

TROUT HILL, C. H. (Postoffice address, Wayne C. H.) —On Twelve Pole river. Ceredo, on the railroad, once settled by a New England colony, dispersed during the war.

WEBSTER.—Headwaters of Elk and Gauley rivers. On turnpike from Tygarts Valley to Nicholas C. H., and on one of the locations of the W. Va. Central R. R. Crossed from east to west by a number of narrow parallel valleys separated by high ridges, which impede communication in a north and south direction. Good roads would make this an attractive county. Uplands and table lands of good surface and soil in large tracts, can be had at from $0.75 to 1.50 per acre, unimproved farms in the valleys from $5 to 10, mountain farms at still lower price. Bituminous coal, and indications of iron ore. Salt was formerly manufactured here.

ADDISON (P. O. address Webster C. H,)—Distant from Sutton, Braxton county, about 30 miles and the same distance from the probable location of the Monongahela and Lewisburg R. R. in Pocahontas county.

WETZEL.—Ohio river, Fishing creek, B. & O. R. R. and turnpike roads. Surface and soil similar to Tyler, adjoining county, and nearly the same amount and value of improvements and production. Timber on rough unimproved lands derives value from proximity of both railroad and river, price from $3 to 10, improved from $10 to 100 per acre. Railroad stations, Burton and Littleton. Postoffices 12.

MARTINSVILLE, C. H.—Ohio river, mouth of Fishing Creek, is a small but thrifty place, 15 miles below Wheeling.

WIRT.—Little Kanawha river, West Fork, Spring, Reedy and Tucker creeks, and turnpikes. Hilly and in part rough. Fine valley lands on the river and some distance up Reedy and Tucker creeks. Soil generally rich. Improvements good. The oil belt extends through this county, embracing the principal development, at Burning Springs, (see Petroleum, page 139.) Iron ore and perhaps other minerals, but little or no coal so far discovered. Price of farming land, improved $10 to 30, unimproved $2.50 to 5 per acre.

ELIZABETH, (P. O. address, Wirt C. H.)—A well located active village, 22 m. distant from Parkersburg and 10 miles from Walkers station, on railroad. Weekly paper, "The Wirt Co. Democrat." The postoffices are Reedy Ripple, Newark, Leachville and Rathbone (Burning Springs) the latter place connects with Parkersburg by telegraph.

WOOD.—Ohio and Little Kanawha rivers, B. & O. R. R. Northwestern, Staunton and other turnpike roads. Very wide and fertile Ohio river bottoms in a good state of cultivation. On the Little Kanawha and some distance up the principal branches the valleys are wide, hills low and easily cultivated, but the soil in part naturally inferior, and in part reduced by overcropping, yet easily improved. Hill land and valleys higher up streams, southward, are more fertile, with a large proportion of limestone soil. Northern part of the county a good clay loam, rolling surface. Oil Belt crosses the eastern end of the county, on brauches of Walker's creek, (see Petroleum, page 139.) The county is well provided with roads; has 5 rail road stations and 19 postoffices. New England, and German settlements. Improved land $12 to $35 per acre inland, other $50 to 100 and adjoining Parkersburg $150 to 300 per acre; unimproved $7 to 12 per acre.

PARKERSBURG, C. H.—At the mouth of Little Kanawha river, and the connection of Balt. & Ohio, and Marietta & Cincinnati railroads. Has a population of 8000, of whieh 5000, together with a large portion of the wealth realized in petroleum production and oil land speculation was added since 1864. Site unsurpassed on the Ohio river for a large commercial and manufacturing city, (see Manufacturing, page 152.) 3 banks: First, Second and Parkersburg National, aggregate capital $300,000. U. S. Circuit Court. Newspapers: Daily and Weekly, "The Times." Weekly: "The Parkersburg Gazette," and "State Journal;" semi-monthly: "The Baptist Record." To be be published after April 1st, monthly, "The West Virginia Monitor," devoted to the description and advertising of West Virginia resources, lands, etc.

WYOMING.—Headwaters of Guyandotte river· Flat Top and Cherry Pond Mountains. Taken from Logan, which it resembles in surface, soil and timber. Fine and tolerably well improved valleys on Clear Fork and Indian creek, but generally the hills are high and close together. Soil remarkably rich throughout; climate mild. With good roads this and the adjoinining counties of Logan and McDowell would soon attract immigration. Improved land $5 to 10, unimproved $1 to 3 per acre. Wild lands chiefly owned by non-residents. Postoffices 4. Coal and indications of iron.

OCEANA, C. H.—A new place on Clear Fork, distant about 32 miles from Ches. & Ohio R. R. via Raleigh, C. H.

OMISSIONS IN THE PRECEDING CHAPTER.

NEWSPAPERS.

Greenbrier Independent, weekly, Lewisburg, Greenbrier county.

West Union Herald, weekly, West Union, Doddridge county.

Bethany Guardian, and Millenial, monthly, Bethany, Brooke county.

STATE DIRECTORY.

GOVERNOR.

His Exc,y W. E. STEVENSON.

SECRETARY OF THE STATE.

CAPT. J. M. PIPES.

AUDITOR OF PUBLIC ACCOUNTS.

THOMAS BOGGESS.

STATE TREASURER.

J. A. McCAULEY.

ADJUTANT AND QUARTERMASTER GENERAL.

GEN. T. M. HARRIS.

ATTORNEY GENERAL.

A. B. CALDWELL.

JUDGES SUPREME COURT OF APPEALS.

HON'S. JAS. H. BROWN, L. S. BERKSHIRE, E. MAXWELL.

MEMBERS OF CONGRESS.

U. S. Senate.—HON. WAITMAN. T. WILLEY.
" — " A. I. BOREMAN.
House of Repr. 1st Dist.—GEN. R. I. DUVALL,
" 2d " —HON. JAMES C. McGREW.
" 3d " —GEN. JOHN S. WITCHER.

JUDGES OF STATE COURTS.

1st CIRCUIT—Ohio, Hancock, Brooke, Marshall. Thayer Melvin.

2d CIRCUIT.—Wetzel, Ritchie, Tyler, Doddridge. C. J. Stewart.

3d CIRCUIT.—Monongalia, Taylor, Tucker, Preston. John A. Dille.

4th CIRCUIT.—Harrison, Marion, Barbour, Randolph. T. W. Harrison.

5th CIRCUIT.—Pendleton, Hardy, Grant, Mineral. J. T. Hoke.

6th CIRCUIT.—Hampshire, Morgan, Berkeley, Jefferson. Jos. E. Chapline.

7th CIRCUIT.—Monroe, Pocahontas, Nicholas, Greenbrier N. Harrison.

8th CIRCUIT.—Lewis, Upshur, Braxton Clay, Webster. Robert Irvine.

9th CIRCUIT.—Wirt, Pleasants, Wood. Geo. H. Loomis.

10th CIRCUIT.—Roane, Gilmer, Calhoun, Jackson. R. S.

Brown.

11th CIRCUIT.—Mason, Putnam, Kanawha. J. W. Hoge.

12th CIRCUIT.—Logan, Boone, Wayne, Lincoln, Cabell. Jas. H. Ferguson.

13th CIRCUIT.—Mercer, Fayette, Wyoming, McDowell, Raleigh. J. L. Gillespie.

JUDGES OF UNITED STATES COURT.

U. S. Circuit Court.—HON. S. P. CHASE.

" District Court.—HON. J. J. JACKSON, JR.

LEGISLATURE.

SENATE.

1st District.—Lewis Applegate, of Brooke, and A. Wilson, of Ohio.

2d District.—J. R. Brown, of Wetzel and Doolittle, of Marshall.

3d District.—Wm. B. Crane, of Preston, and J. H. Cather, of Taylor.

4th District.—William I. Boreman, of Tyler, and A. Werninger, of Harrison.

5th District.—James Cather, of Gilmer, and G. K. Leonard, of Wood.

6th District.—Spencer Dayton, of Barbour, and D. D. T. Farnsworth, of Upshur.

7th District.—Dr. Spicer Patrick, of Kanawha, and J. M. Phelps, of Mason.

8th District.—Mitchell Cook, of Wyoming, and Z. D. Ramsdell, of Wayne.

9th District,—Alex. H. Humphreys, of Monroe, and S. Young, of Pocahontas.

10th District.—George F. Harman, of Grant, and H. Davis, of Mineral.

11th District.—George Koonce, of Jefferson, and Samuel Gold, of Berkeley.

Hon. D. D. T. Farnsworth, President. E. W. S. Moore, Clerk.

HOUSE OF DELEGATES.

Barbour—Joseph Teter.
Berkeley—John W. Lamon and J. D. Ropp.
Boone—F. W. Meadows.
Braxton— Alpheus W. McCoy.
Brooke—James Hervey.
Doddridge—Floyd Neely.
Preston—Asbury C. Baker, and John Collins.
Putnam—J. T. Bowyer.
Ritchie—Noah Rexroad.
Roane—William Gandee.
Taylor—Reuben Davisson.
Tyler—Selman Wells.
Upshur—T. G. Farnsworth.

Fayette—R. A. Flanagan.
Hampshire—A. H. Pownall.
Hancock—Daniel Doneboo.
Harrison—Nathan Goff and John J. Davis.
Jackson—F. R. Hassler.
Jefferson—Jacob J. Miller and George M. Beltzhoover.
Kanawha—Benj'n H. Smith and A. E. Summers.
Lewis—Henry Brannon.
Logan—Rhodes D. Ballard.
Marion—Francis H. Peirpoint and Robert M. Hill.
Marshall—E. C. Thomas and Wm. R. Howe.
Mason—Hiram R. Howard.
Mercer—George Evans.
Mineral—Wm. M. Welch.
Monongalia—William Price and George C. Sturgiss.
Morgan—Joseph C. Wheat.
Ohio—Daniel Lamb, E. C. Cracraft and Faris.
Pendleton—W. H. H. Flick.
Wetzel—James Guthrie.
Wayne—Goble C. Bargess.
Wirt—Charles B. Fisher.
1st Del. Dist—(Wood and Pleasants) Jas. M. Jackson and J. M. Agnew.
2d Del. Dist—(Calhoun and Gilmer) George Lynch.
3d Del. Dist—(Clay and Nicholas. M. Rader.
4th Del. Dist—(Pocahontas and Webster) N. G. Barlow.
5th Del. Dist—(Randolph and Tucker) Rufus Maxwell.
6th Del. Dist—(Raleigh, Wyoming and McDowell) James Scott.
7th Del. Dist—(Grant and Hardy) Martin Judy.
8th Del. Dist—(Cabell and Lincoln) J. A. Wilkinson.
Greenbrier and Monroe (together)—B. F. Ballard, Rufus A. Chambers and George W. Carpenter.

Wm. M. Welch, Speaker. W. P. Hubbard, Clerk.

WEST VIRGINIA HOSPITAL FOR INSANE.

President of the Board of Directors. Hon. N. Goff, Clarksburg

---

BOARD OF REGENTS W. VA. UNIVERSITY.

T. H. Logan, Hon, F. H. Peirpoint, George M. Hogans, Samuel Billingsley, Hon. A. I. Boreman, Hon. J. Loomis Gould, W. W. Harper, Mark Poore, Hon. Samuel Young, Hon. James Carskadon, Hon. J. T. Hoke.

STATE SUPERINTENDENT OF FREE SCHOOLS.

H. A. G. ZIEGLER.

COMMISSIONER OF IMMIGRATION.

J. H. DISS DEBAR, Parkersburg.

www.ingramcontent.com/pod-product-compliance
Lightning Source LLC
LaVergne TN
LVHW011218110826
845150LV00006B/1466

9781425516482